Bor
Personality Disorder

Everything You Need To Know About
Borderline Personality Disorder

By Richard Smith

Copyright 2015 by Richard Smith.

Published by Make Profits Easy LLC

Profitsdaily123@aol.com

facebook.com/MakeProfitsEasy

Table of Contents

Introduction

There has always been a stigma attached to people who are considered mentally ill. They are referred to by society as "crazy", "hysteric", or simply those that lack the discipline to make a better life for themselves. Many people don't understand that people who are diagnosed with mental disorders are going through a struggle that is very real; they are going through a serious ordeal.

Mental illness spares no one: children, adolescents, adults, and even the elderly. Chances are, you may have a friend, parent, sibling, relative, coworker, or spouse who has it. When a loved one is affected, it changes the dynamic of the relationships we have.

Oftentimes, psychiatric disorders are powerful enough to wreak havoc on the entire household simply because people don't know enough about it, and how to deal with it. When these issues aren't addressed properly, it can lead to a painful cycle of blame and hurt.

The most common mental illness is borderline personality disorder (BPD), which affects 2% of the American population each year. It is characterized by the inability to maintain stable personal relationships and extremely impulsive behavior; which is why it is commonly referred to as emotionally unstable personality disorder or emotional intensity disorder, among others. Symptoms of borderline personality disorder usually manifest themselves during adolescence or early childhood, but it can also occur later in life for others. BPD is associated with self-harm and suicide, but when diagnosed and treated early on the prognosis is quite good.

If you want to know more about borderline personality disorder, you've come to the right place. By reading this book, you will learn all the aspects surrounding this mysterious yet common illness:

- Symptoms of borderline personality disorder
- Conventional and alternative treatment options
- Living with someone who has BPD
- How to communicate with someone who has BPD
- The impact of BPD in families
- How to convince your child to get treatment
- Choosing the right therapist
- How family and friends can help loved ones with BPD

If you or someone you love has BPD, you will find all the information needed to cope with this illness. It is not impossible to overcome, but it is most important to arm yourself with information.

Chapter 1: History of Borderline Personality Disorder and the Causes of It

The first known cases of borderline personality disorder symptoms were recorded in medical literature that dates back 3,000 years ago. In 1938, it was Adolph Stern, an American psychoanalyst who officially described the symptoms of BPD which we know today as the diagnostic criteria. He was also responsible for initially suggesting the causes of BPD and made recommendations on the most effective forms of psychotherapy for treatment. Adolph Stern was also responsible for naming the disorder by classifying patients that met the diagnostic criteria as a border line group.

Another psychoanalyst by the name of Robert Knight introduced ego psychology into the description of BPD during the 1940's. Ego psychology dealt with the mental functions which affect how people see events in their life and how we respond to these situations around us. It was also Robert Knight who suggested that people suffering from borderline disorder are impaired in ego psychology since they encounter difficulties in reacting normally. He referred to these cases as borderline states.

Otto Kernberg made a significant contribution to the field of psychology when, in the 1960's, he suggested that mental disorders were affected by three aspects of personality: neurotic, psychotic, and borderline. He was also known for proposing modified psychoanalytic therapy for patients of BPD.

In 1968, the first research on borderline disorder was conducted by Roy Grinker and his colleagues. In the study he referred to BPD as borderline syndrome. In 1979, a group of doctors namely Bernard Beitman, John Brinkley, and Robert Friedel suggested that medications are effective in the treatment of borderline symptoms. These medications are known today as antipsychotic agents. This led to numerous studies investigating the effectiveness of medications in reducing symptoms of borderline disorder.

During the 1980's, it was first discovered that borderline disorder is linked to biological disturbances in the brain. This discovery was made possible through the use of biochemical and genetic studies combined with neuroimaging.

In 1993, Marsha Linehan pioneered the most widely used form of treatment today known as Dialectical Behavior Therapy. It is now a well-documented and established method of treatment for borderline personality disorder particularly for those who are prone to self-harm and suicide. Since Marsha Linehan's development of DBT, other forms of psychotherapy have been developed primarily for the treatment of BPD.

What Causes Borderline Personality Disorder?

The exact causes of borderline personality disorder are not established, although this is an area that doctors continue to study. Experts in the field do agree that there are certain contributing factors, both environmental and biological, that increase a person's risk of developing borderline personality disorder. These are:

1. Genetics: Studies have shown that over 60% of those diagnosed with borderline personality disorder suffer from genetic abnormalities that affect the brain's pathways responsible for cognitive activity, impulse control, and the way the brain processes emotions. This is the reason why BPD is manifested by a lack of logical perception and reasoning.

While it is agreed that there isn't a single gene that is responsible for the development of borderline personality disorder, it is also hereditary as it can be passed down from one generation to another. First degree relatives, including parents, children, or siblings of those who have BPD, are 10 times more likely to be diagnosed with the same disorder some time in their lives. Borderline personality disorder studies that have focused on twins also confirmed that the illness is hereditary. People can inherit temperament and other personality traits which include aggression and impulsiveness.

2. Brain abnormalities: The brains of those who have borderline personality disorder share common characteristics:

- The hippocampus, which makes up a significant part of the limbic system which regulates emotions, is smaller in those who have BPD. The same feature is also observed in those who suffer from post-traumatic stress disorder.

- The amygdala may also be smaller and more active for those diagnosed with BPD. The amygdala is an almond-sized set of neurons in the brain, responsible for processing emotions both positive and negative. The unusually strong activity in the amygdala may be the reason why those with BPD exhibit more heightened negative emotions including shame, fear, anger, and sadness.

- The prefrontal cortex, responsible for decision making, personality expression, complex cognitive behavior, and social behavior, is less active in those who have BPD. In particular it is less active when the patient is observed as they are recalling feelings of fear and abandonment. Since the prefrontal cortex is responsible for stimulating emotions, the inactivity in this part of the brain could be the primary reason why those with BPD have difficulties controlling their emotions and managing stress.

- The hypothalamic-pituitary-adrenal axis which is responsible for cortisol production, is more active in those who have borderline personality disorder. Cortisol is released as the body's response to stress, and an increase of it in the body may result to higher incidence of irritability which is observed in those who have BPD. If a person has experienced traumatic events in their past, this may also lead to increased cortisol production.

3. Environmental factors: A person's behavior is shaped by their experiences in life; particularly in relation to one's childhood as well as the relationships with parents or families as a whole. While various environmental factors may be responsible for borderline personality disorder,

the most critical always seems to be poor parenting. A child who experiences separation from one or both parents, who experienced physical, verbal, or sexual abuse by a family member, or who received little to no care, are at high risk for developing borderline personality disorder.

However, it is still important to note that children who do not experience abuse or traumas within their family can still develop borderline personality disorder. In this scenario, biological causes are at play and are significant enough to cause BPD.

4. Estrogen: Varying estrogen levels in women may also be responsible for causing borderline personality disorder. The effects of estrogen on the brain chemistry of women's reproductive hormones are very complex. This is because estrogen levels can lead to a fluctuation of other hormones. Examples of these include:

- A decrease in dopamine levels, the neurotransmitter responsible for reward, memory, and behavior;

- Varying effects on serotonin levels, which is responsible for producing feelings of happiness and well-being;

- Increased production of endorphins in the brain and the blood, which is responsible for feelings of euphoria and inhibiting the transmission of pain signals;

- Increased norepinephrine levels, which contracts the heart as a response to stress

Studies have shown that BPD symptoms exhibited by women changed according to their menstrual cycle due to the estrogen levels in their bodies. This is a reason why women who suffer from pre-menstrual syndrome are often misdiagnosed for borderline personality disorder. They exhibit the same characteristics such as extreme mood swings, depression, sadness, and irritability.

5. Society and Culture: People who live in societies with higher incidences of unstable family relationships are more prone to developing borderline personality disorder. The combination of poor lifestyle choices, impulsiveness, and other symptoms of BPD increases a person's chances for risky situations. For this reason, adults who live with BPD are more vulnerable to being victims of rape, violence, as well as other crimes.

6. Child Abuse: There are different kinds of child abuse and neglect that contribute to borderline

personality disorder. Physical abuse occurs when a caregiver or parent hurts a child with the intention of injury. Disciplinary measures that entail a physical aspect is not considered to be child abuse if the child does not have an injury.

Sexual abuse is when a child is forced to engage in sexual behavior, not limited to fondling or assault. Other acts that constitute sexual abuse include occasions when an adult exposes their genitals to a child, takes photographs of a child as they are naked with the intent of using it for sexual purposes, or forces a child to engage in sex.

Emotional abuse can come in the form of withholding love, insults, threats, and constant criticism. Emotional abuse does not leave visible scars unlike physical abuse. However, emotional abuse can harm a person psychologically for a long period of time.

Neglect is also a form of child abuse and occurs when a parent or caregiver is unable to meet a child's basic needs including shelter, food, education, safety, and emotional support. When a child is left alone without proper adult supervision this also constitutes neglect.

Chapter 2: Symptoms of Borderline Personality Disorder

The primary signs that a person may be suffering from borderline personality disorder is an evident pattern of unstable personal relationships, negative self-image, and being too emotional. People with BPD are also usually very impulsive and may resort to self-destructive behavior such as suicide attempts and risky sexual behavior. Symptoms of BPD are consistent and observed in a wide range of social as well as personal situations. Eventually, if left untreated, these can lead to added stress and inability to function properly in social and work situations. The patterns are also noticeable because they are stable and tend to be long in duration.

1. **Emotional Instability:** BPD is also referred to as Emotionally Unstable Disorder because it is the prevalent characteristic in most cases. This is characterized as impulsivity, a rapid shift in emotions, chaotic relationships, and hostility. It is also common for people with BPD to jump from one emotional crisis to another.

While most people tend to experience impulsivity and rapid mood shifts during adolescence, those with borderline personality disorder exhibit it later in life although it will last for a longer period of time. Adults who have BPD tend to suffer from extreme mood swings and anger. It is also normal for people to experience occasional mood shifts and emotional changes but for those who have BPD, these episodes are much more intense that it will impact their work, social, and personal lives.

Those with borderline personality disorder also have other problems with emotions. They tend to feel more negative emotions than other people. They also feel more "empty" and in fact may even describe the feeling as though they have nothing inside.

People with borderline personality disorder also feel emotions more intensely than others. It is not uncommon to meet people with BPD who live generally joyful and happy lives, but when they encounter negative emotions they instantly feel overwhelmed. Examples of these are instead of feeling sadness, they feel grief; instead of feeling embarrassed they feel humiliation and shame; instead of being annoyed they experience rage; and instead of feeling nervous they panic. For this reason, people with BPD are extremely sensitive to feelings associated with failure, isolation, and rejection.

Since they are not able to cope with these intense emotions they may result to self-harm. People with BPD are aware of the fact that they are having difficulties dealing with negative emotions and because they are unable to find an outlet to cope they try to shut off these emotions completely.

Mood swings are part of the emotional instability experienced by individuals who have borderline personality disorder. These mood swings can happen often, in fact someone with BPD may go through many episodes in the course of a day. On the other hand, a mentally healthy person will experience mood swings just twice in a week. The mood swings brought about by borderline personality disorder are consistent over time.

There are also distinguishing features of mood swings caused by BPD. The primary difference is that BPD mood swings are caused by triggers, usually when the trigger is related to perceived rejection by another person. However, if a person is suffering from mood swings alone it is not enough to diagnose them of borderline personality disorder since it is just one of the many symptoms.

2. **Impulsive behavior:** Impulsive behavior is common in people with borderline personality disorder. It refers to acting quickly on something without contemplating the consequences of one's actions. Acting on impulse is usually a response to an event that causes extreme emotions that are usually negative, but for those with borderline personality disorder they act impulsively as a way to deal with their emotions.

It provides them with immediate relief from pain.

Common characteristics include alcohol or substance abuse, risky sexual behavior include participation in unprotected sex with multiple partners, reckless driving, irresponsible spending, and eating disorders. They also tend to change jobs and leave relationships more often. While it is normal for people to participate in these impulsive activities occasionally, for those with BPD it lasts for a longer period of time because they see these activities as an attempt to restore some normalcy in their lives and respond to extreme emotion. Impulsive behavior is one of the most troubling aspects of borderline personality disorder because it can lead to severe health problems, relationship issues, financial woes, and even legal issues down the line.

People with borderline personality disorder also experience feelings of shame and guilt after giving into their impulsive behavior. It is a dangerous cycle that involves feeling extreme emotions, resorting to impulsive behavior as way of relieving their pain, then immediately feeling shameful and guilty about their behavior, resulting in emotional pain. This all leads to more extreme emotional pain to which a person with BPD will resort to new impulsive behavior in order to cope with their new pain. Over time, impulsive behavior will become an automatic way of dealing with emotional pain. This cycle explains why many people with borderline personality disorder tend to become addicted to different things that give them temporary relief from their emotions. For the same reason it is also why addiction and impulsivity in borderline personality disorder overlaps.

The common characteristics of people suffering from addiction and borderline personality disorder include:

- Impulsive and harmful behavior
- Severe mood swings ranging from depression and feelings of joy
- Manipulative actions
- A lack of concern for one's health and safety
- Pursuing dangerous activity despite the high risks involved
- A pattern of instability in finances, relationships, and jobs

The relationship between borderline personality disorder and addiction can be rather volatile. Drug and substance abuse will further aggravate the other dangerous symptoms of BPD particularly depression and anger. In some cases, this leads to more profound feelings of emotional emptiness.

Dialectical Behavior Therapy (DBT) is the best course of treatment in addressing this co-occurring disorder. It teaches skills such as mood awareness, meditation exercises, and training in social skills where the end goal is to reduce one's impulsivity. One of the key features of DBT that is useful in treating impulsivity is mindfulness which helps people become more aware of the consequences of the actions they are about to engage in. With the practice of mindfulness, impulsive people take the time to make better informed and healthy decisions as well as have better responses even in the light of extreme emotions and stress.

Some medications may also help reduce the symptoms of impulsivity in a person. However, the drugs are only effective when they are used together with psychotherapy. It should be noted that medication should not be the first course of treatment for impulsivity although it is useful for BPD and other co-occurring disorders. Antidepressants such as selective serotonin reuptake inhibitors are effective in treating impulsive behavior that occurs with borderline personality disorder. Other medicines such as Effexor and Serzone have been shown to reduce symptoms of impulsivity.

3. **Unstable Relationships:** People suffering from BPD are not capable of having stable personal relationships. They cannot be alone for

long periods of time because they also tend to suffer from abandonment anxiety. People with borderline personality disorder will try to hide their manipulative characteristics and dependency on their partners.

The inability to have lasting, stable relationships is also connected to impulsive behavior stemming from borderline personality behavior. Promiscuity and substance abuse creates conflict with romantic partners, resulting in separation, divorce, and even domestic violence.

People who suffer from BPD have difficulty trusting other people. They feel irritable and angry, exhibiting temper tantrums even toward people that they care for. Because people with borderline personality disorder have a distorted view of what is socially acceptable, they experience difficulty in trusting people and cooperating with others. If they experience challenges within their relationships, they don't respond in a manner that would help to repair it unlike others. Doing this severely limits their capacity to be fully cooperative in romantic relationships as well as friendships.

The main reason why people with borderline personality disorder find it difficult to focus on the emotions of other people is because they themselves are too overwhelmed with their own feelings. They find that their emotional pain is a major obstacle. Individuals with borderline personality disorder also tend to feel that regardless of what their partner does, their emotional needs are never met. In spite of this, they don't have the ability to assert what they need in a healthy, productive manner. This results in frustrations because at the end of the day they don't get what they want and they feel angry.

People with BPD lack the skills to manage their anger and end up lashing out at their partners. Many cases of sexual and physical aggression towards partners are associated to borderline personality disorder.

Additionally, individuals with BPD view relationships as black or white. For them, people are either all good or all bad, there is no middle ground. In relationships, this kind of mentality devalues one's partners. But since they have extreme fears of abandonment, they may also resort to manipulation to prevent their partners from leaving them.

In particular, men who have borderline personality disorder can be emotionally explosive. Men with BPD are usually jealous, depressive, and angry most of the time. They may resort to physical aggression once they feel that their female partners are placing a distance between them, whether socially or emotionally.

This kind of behavior is also observed in lesbian relationships wherein one partner is suffering from borderline personality disorder. These situations found one partner resorting to violence when they felt that their partner was becoming physically or emotionally distant in the relationship. Studies have also shown that women with BPD are at higher risk of using aggression in relationships than those without BPD.

Couples wherein one partner suffers from borderline personality disorder usually have to turn to counseling as a form of therapy. It is necessary for each person in the relationship to see a therapist separately from the other so that they can each work on their own issues followed by addressing the relationship as a whole. There are therapists specializing in borderline personality disorder who can help couples manage their relationships better and move forward despite BPD.

4. **Identity disturbance:** People with BPD don't have a stable secure personality or sense of self. They are more sensitive to their environment and the people that they spend time with. As a result they will end up adopting habits, values, and even mimicking the attitudes of the people they spend time with the most.

Identity disturbance is also characterized by sudden but intense changes in a person's image.

The instability in one's identity can also result to dramatic changes in career, values, life goals, types of friends, sexual identity, and even opinions.

5. **Paranoia:** In some cases, people with borderline personality disorder also suffer from paranoia. They are overtly suspicious of other people's behaviors and intentions, sometimes feeling like everyone is out to get them. These episodes of paranoia may come and go, and are usually short lived. At most, it can last for a few days and often occur in periods of distress or trauma. People with paranoia tend to think that the world is out to get them, and have fears that include people spying on them or that friends are talking behind their back.

Paranoid thinking can be mild and short lived, although there are people that experience severe paranoia that lasts for months. Individuals that suffer from delusional disorder or psychotic disorders have chronic, severe paranoia which is completely unrelated from anything going on in reality.

6. **Fears of Abandonment:** Unlike separation anxiety, people with BPD experience abandonment fears wherein they perceive separation or a change in routine in their near future. This will cause them to react by extreme changes in behavior, self-image, thought, and mannerisms. If the thought of abandonment

traumatizes them, they may resort to self-harm and even attempt suicide as a means of coping.

Most people with BPD who suffer from abandonment issues don't realize it but their behavior tells it all. There are certain characteristics of people with BPD that are related to their fear of abandonment. These include:

- Staying in an unhealthy relationship because they cannot overcome their fear of being alone. Oftentimes people with BPD have extreme fears of abandonment that even if they are in a dysfunctional relationship that does not benefit them in any way whatsoever, they refuse to get out of it as they have formed a dependency on their partner. As a result both partners end up staying in a relationship that is full of conflict and drama.

- Fear of abandonment may also be manifested through depression because the sadness is turned inwards.

- People who have abandonment issues may show rage to people that they love. While it sounds like the complete opposite behavior you would expect from someone who does not want to be left by a loved one, people with BPD feel vulnerable and helpless and may end up lashing at their partner to regain a sense of control.

- It is common for partners to experience being harassed by their partners who have BPD. It may be in the form of being bombarded by phone calls, texts, and emails because a person with BPD constantly needs reassurance that they will not be abandoned. Furthermore, fear of abandonment causes people to find solitude or isolation completely unbearable and constantly trying to be in contact with their partner.

The cause of abandonment issues in people with borderline personality disorder varies. For some, it may be traumatic childhood issues that stemmed from neglect or abuse by a caregiver. Children who have been adopted, experienced the separation of their parents, or had a loved one die are also more prone to abandonment issues later on.

7. **Anger:** Most people with borderline personality disorder feel angry all the time. They may or may not express it, but the feelings of anger or rage are there. Their anger may be caused by a variety of factors but primarily it is a result of feeling neglected, ignored, or uncared

for especially by people they are close to. People with BPD may also feel shameful or guilty if they express their anger.

8. **Dissociation:** Defined as a form of attachment that leaves a person feeling unreal and numb, dissociation usually occurs on its own. Everyone can experience dissociation at some point in their lives, where they feel like they just went on automatic pilot in a particular situation. Because borderline personality disorder is considered a dissociative disorder, it gives the feeling that one is merely going through the motions of life without actually having any control. People who experience dissociation end up doing things without feeling emotions or connecting to the situation or people at all. In conditions of extreme dissociation, people can sometimes experience a complete block in memory. They are unable to recall situations where they encountered trauma, abuse, and major stress as a survival mechanism.

For some people, the intensity of BPD symptoms doesn't last and in fact may decrease over time. This may be attributed to age, although there is no explanation yet on why some symptoms remain and others decline. There are some theories that attempt to explain this:

- Treatment and knowledge of borderline personality disorder can greatly reduce the symptoms' intensity through the years. This is an obvious reason, as people who receive treatment and learn how to improve their lifestyles eventually reduce the problems they encountered before which was a result of BPD behavior.

- Burn out may also occur as BPD symptoms lessen with age. It is also a fact that individuals with borderline personality disorder just engage in less impulsive activities.

- People with BPD may also reduce interpersonal relationships altogether after many years of conflict and drama. Simply put, they avoid forming relationships to avoid problems.

Despite the observable decline of BPD symptoms in people as they age, there is no substitute for treatment. It is not a reason for people to avoid seeking help, thinking that things will improve in time. BPD people already put their lives in enough risk with impulsive behavior and miss out living their lives to their full potential.

9. **Self-harm:** Self-harm is a common symptom in people with borderline personality disorder. However, it is not to be confused with suicide because the two are completely different. Individuals resort to self-harm as a method of numbing emotional pain or as a way of

punishing themselves. People also engage in self-harm as a way of reducing suicidal thoughts. In some cases, people with BPD fear that if they stop giving in to the urges to harm themselves they may actually become suicidal.

10. **Suicide:** Almost 80% of people with BPD have attempted suicide at least once in their lifetime. Unfortunately, around 10% of these people will actually succeed at their suicide attempt. This is why it is necessary for those with a higher suicidal risk to be treated with inpatient methods and be confined in hospitals where they will be detached from anything that they can use to harm themselves.

Chapter 3: Co-Occurring Disorders

Borderline personality disorder may also occur simultaneously with other mental health issues wherein one symptom can influence the outcome and treatment of the illness. These situations are referred to as comorbidities.

1. **Depression:** The most common comorbidity of borderline personality disorder is depression. More than 80% of those with BPD are also depressive. This is because borderline personality disorder and depression share the same biological features, placing those with BPD at higher risk for depression.

In fact, symptoms of extreme depressive episodes may be observed in individuals with BPD. Examples of these include constant irritability, depressed moods, and a decreased interest in activities that previously were enjoyable to them. Major depression is also characterized by significant changes in weight.

This comorbidity also has an impact on one's sleeping patterns, as people suffering from these disorders report having a more difficult time falling asleep or staying asleep which leads to fatigue. In general, they also have decreased energy and lack of physical activity which are major symptoms of depressive episodes. There is an increase in worry, feeling agitated, shameful, and guilty.

Negative affect plays a significant role in major depressive disorder and borderline personality disorder. This is characterized by serenity and calmness on one end of the spectrum, and nervousness and hostility on the other end. People with the high positive affect maintain active, energetic lives while those who have the low positive affect are usually more sluggish and drowsy. The intensity of the affect is related to symptoms of depression, which is why the relationship between the two mental health disorders can somehow be explained by the affect. Individuals who suffer from both BPD and depression experience an inability to regulate emotions so the combination of high negative effects can be disastrous.

In some cases, people who are suffering from both borderline personality disorder and depression have slower response rates to treatment as compared to those who suffer from depression alone. However, research also shows that when a patient has both BPD and depression but receives treatment for BPD, depression is also usually reduced.

When borderline personality disorder and depression are co-occurring, licensed medical professionals have the capacity to provide the proper treatment which usually consists of antidepressants combined with various behavioral techniques.

2. **Eating disorders:** The incidence of eating disorders in those with mental illnesses is much higher as compared to the incidence of mental disorders in the general population. What's more is that the percentage of those with BPD who also have eating disorders is much higher than the prevalence of personality disorder which is quite alarming. A significant percentage of those who have anorexia and bulimia are actually also suffering from borderline personality disorder.

Anorexia is characterized by a refusal to maintain a healthy body weight, or in extreme cases when a person weighs less than 80% of their normal weight for their age and size. Anorexic individuals usually accomplish this goal by starving themselves, and by eating so little that they can go for days without eating a full meal. Despite being severely underweight, anorexics feel panic at the mere thought of gaining weight. They also deny the gravity of being underweight. Health issues that arise as a side effect of anorexia include reproductive complications, cardiovascular problems, and gastrointestinal dysfunction.

Bulimia nervosa occurs when one resorts to binge eating usually in a discrete location where they can consume excessively large amounts of food which are more than what a normal person would consume. They do this in hidden locations away from the eyes of other people. To prevent weight gain from binge eating, those who have bulimia then resort to compensatory behaviors which includes the use of laxatives, forced vomiting, enemas, diuretics, excessive exercise, and medications. This cycle of binge eating and compensatory behaviors may occur twice a week on average.

There are two kinds of bulimia: the purging and non-purging types. Those who fall under the purging category use laxatives and vomiting to prevent weight gain despite binge eating. On the other hand, non-purging types use excessive exercise and fasting to keep their weight down. Bulimia can result in serious consequences such as electrolyte and fluid damage, constipation, irritable bowel syndrome, and the decay of teeth because of vomiting.

Binge eating is also another form of eating disorder that plagues people who have BPD. It is characterized by episodes of binge eating followed by a sense of guilt because they had lost complete control during eating.

It is observed that a person's gender may affect the kind of comorbidity that occurs with borderline personality disorder. Women with BPD are more prone to developing eating disorders, while men are vulnerable to substance abuse. Similarly, it is also women who tend to develop post-traumatic stress disorder, anxiety issues, and mood swings rather than men.

Symptoms of personality disorders are usually manifested during adolescence because a person may have experienced various life stressors that triggered a change in temperament. Scientists observe that mental health problems occur before a person succumbs to eating disorders when comorbidities occur. This is the reason why it is necessary to clearly understand the relationship between a co-occurring disorder and a personality disorder so that these may be addressed and treated effectively.

Many other psychological and biological risk factors also play a part in causing eating disorders. A child whose parents often commented on their image, size, or weight in a negative light clearly contributed to the distortion of a healthy body image. Furthermore, constant criticism or negative commenting definitely play a role as a stressor. Borderline personality disorder is also characterized by disturbed identities as well as fears of abandonment, features that tend to shape the kind of comorbidity that occurs. People with BPD are extremely impulsive individuals, a characteristic that can trigger eating disorders as a comorbidity in the form of binge eating. Additionally, the self-harming characteristics are also displayed by forcing oneself to vomit and abusing laxatives.

People with BPD who also suffer from eating disorders view controlling food and body image as a way of satisfying empty feelings that are common with the illness. Food acts as a platform for which they can control and forget the negative feelings that they experience. Activities such as purging may also be seen as a form of relief for those with borderline personality disorder, because this very act results in fatigue thereby calming down intense angry emotions.

If someone you care about has both borderline personality disorder and also suffers from an eating disorder, there are things that you can do to help them cope.

- Recognize that eating disorders are a mental illness, and avoid telling them to stop giving in to it and act normal instead. While eating disorders are abnormal, telling them to stop doing what they are doing will not help. This may have the opposite effect because it shows insensitivity on your part. When a person resorts to starving themselves or binge eating, this problem is deeply psychological and requires professional medical help to cure.

- Read up on the eating disorder that your loved one is plagued with. Just like with other psychiatric disorders, it is necessary to stay informed on what a family member, spouse, or friend is going through in order for you to understand the situation better.

- Emphasize the positive aspects of the relationship. Just because your loved one has an eating disorder is no reason for you to focus on it solely because it is causing a strain in the relationship. It is necessary to stay balanced and keep in mind that the other person is struggling to cope with having a normal life. Eating disorders are their outlet for dealing with emotions, so it would not help to pinpoint the negative aspects all the time.

- Encourage your loved one to get treatment for their eating disorder. Show them that you care about them and let them know that professional treatment can help them overcome their struggles.

3. **Substance Abuse:** There is a clear correlation between mental illnesses and substance abuse, as proven time and again in countless scientific studies. Simply put, the mere

presence of a psychiatric illness in a person will immediately make them more susceptible to substance abuse. Because of this, the longer the illness goes untreated, the more a person is at risk for substance dependence for a longer period of time. Substances may vary, with the popular forms being alcohol, cocaine, cannabis, and other opiates.

However, risk levels vary depending on the kind of personality disorder. This means that the risk for substance dependence is not equal among people who are suffering from mental health problems. Anxiety disorders also place people at risk for substance abuse, and this risk is not the same as those with people suffering from personality disorders. Studies show that patients who are dependent on substances suffer from personality disorders too but antisocial personality is the most common disorder while BPD comes in second.

Almost half of all patients being treated for borderline personality disorder have had a history of substance abuse, which can last anywhere from a few months to a lifetime if left untreated.

The major problem with substance abuse as a comorbidity in people with borderline personality disorder is that it will add on to the problems. Individuals with BPD who are also dependent on substances will be more impulsive and suffer from more extreme relationship issues and general instability in life.

Younger people with borderline personality disorder are predisposed to developing substance abuse as a comorbidity. Both disorders share the same risk factors, particularly childhood trauma. However, one interesting theory is that borderline personality disorders lead to substance abuse and vice versa. To cite an example, since drug abuse depletes a person's brain of serotonin this causes them to be impulsive and more prone to self-destructive behaviors. This behavior makes them neurologically prone to developing BPD and therefore also more responsive to the temporary highs of substance abuse.

Alcohol and drug dependence results in the loss of valuable interpersonal relationships in people. When this happens, a person suffering from substance abuse may develop symptoms that resemble borderline personality disorder. Some studies also show that people with BPD turn to substances as a way to medicate as it gives them a temporary outlet to calm down from all the anger and intense feelings that they experience in their daily lives. The use of drugs provides a sense of stability, and helps patients of BPD regulate their emotions.

The temporary benefits will differ for people with borderline personality disorder depending on their substance of choice. The most widely abused substance is alcohol, which acts as a relaxant. It is a nervous system depressant because of its sedative properties and is often used by those who experience constricted emotions or who feel trapped. By consuming alcohol, they are able to get rid of distressed feelings and reduce their normally defensive states.

Cocaine is a drug that makes a person feel more energetic and confident while decreasing fatigue. It gives the feeling of an elevated mood and may also help increase productivity. However, scientists report that there are two kinds of cocaine users: high energy and low energy. Those that derive high energy from cocaine use feel positive, sometimes even elated. On the other hand, low energy cocaine users feel fatigued and bored. Regardless of which category a person falls under, cocaine users are known to turn to the drug in order to relieve themselves from restlessness, boredom, and emptiness.

Opiates in all forms are designed to reduce pain. A significant majority of individuals with borderline personality disorder are addicted to various types of opiates. Consuming opiates is a form of adaptation which allows a person with BPD to silence their internal rage that resulted from experiencing aggression or violence early in life. For the same reason, those suffering from post-traumatic stress disorder are also prone to opiate abuse.

On the other hand, people with both BDP and alcoholism have tend to suffer from more difficulties in their lives and are less receptive to treatment as compared to those who only have one of the disorders. Those who have both alcoholism and BPD are more likely to stay in treatment centers for substance abuse for a longer period of time and tend to have more suicidal tendencies. Additionally they are also more prone to other kinds of harmful behavior such as gambling, binge eating, and other addictive patterns.

There are many factors that explain the high co-occurrence of alcoholism with borderline personality disorder. The first of these is that both disorders have common genetic pathways. This means that the same genes that put people at higher risk for alcoholism also make them more vulnerable to developing symptoms of BPD. Both disorders also stem from the same environmental causes such as childhood abuse, maltreatment, and abandonment from a parent or caregiver early in life. Another link between the two is that those who suffer from BPD use alcohol to numb themselves from the intense emotions that is brought about by BPD.

4. **Trauma:** It is a known fact that childhood traumas increase the risk for developing severe

psychological issues in adolescence or adulthood. Trauma can cause mental health issues such as depression, substance abuse, panic disorder, eating disorder, and post-traumatic stress disorder. Many of the known mental health issues manifest themselves as a result of experiencing traumas during childhood.

Trauma may come in various forms: physical, emotional, sexual, or verbal abuse; violence within the family, parental rejection, separation from family, or experiencing a serious illness. All of these have an effect on how a child's sense of self-identity. Maltreatment will also impact a child's sense of attachment, leading to attachment anxiety or attachment avoidance. This type of behavior can carry on to adulthood and is characterized by the need for intimacy coupled with the fear of rejection. Adults that experience trauma seek out intimate relationships but tend to view their partners as dependent, and may often have commitment issues. Personality disorders that may occur later in life as a result of trauma include paranoid behavior, schitzotypal, avoidant, and borderline personality disorder.

Childhood sexual abuse is the most common form of trauma observed in people with borderline personality disorder. Because of its prevalence within the BPD population, researchers believe that the occurrence of childhood sexual abuse to be a major risk factor for developing borderline personality disorder in adulthood. In fact, some cases showed that sexual abuse predicted the development of BPD in individuals even better than family or environment.

Severe dissociation, or the state of being removed from reality, is one of the obvious symptoms that a person has borderline personality disorder. Many doctors theorize that it is tied to the emotional neglect experienced by those who have BPD. Dissociation is displayed through constant daydreaming or spacing out. Childhood trauma is a common factor in many cases of people with dissociation and borderline personality disorder. Individuals allow themselves to space out, or disconnect from reality, as a method of forgetting about childhood traumas.

5. **Avoidance Personality Disorder:**
Avoidance Personality Disorder or APD occurs in 40% of people who have borderline personality disorder. It is defined as consistently feeling inadequate and hypersensitive. People with APD generally avoid situations where they have to engage with other people because they are afraid of being criticized, have low self-esteem, and are preoccupied with thoughts of rejection. Additionally, individuals with APD feel self-conscious, are too critical of themselves, and are

extremely shy. It is a clinical disorder because this kind of behavior has a significant negative impact in one's relationships, career, and other important aspects in life.

BPD and APD are commonly co-occurring disorders because both illnesses share the same dominant trait which is intense fear of rejection and criticism. When a person has this characteristic it increases their chances for developing both BPD and APD.

Among the known treatments for borderline personality disorder, cognitive behavioral therapy seems to be the most effective in addressing avoidance personality disorder.

6. **Antisocial Personality Disorder:** Defined as a pervasive pattern in violating and disregarding the rights of other people, antisocial personality disorder (ASPD) is usually manifested in childhood or adolescence but continues to adulthood. Generally, people who have antisocial personality disorder lack empathy and often break the law. It is also associated with impulsive behavior and aggression. They are described as irresponsible and usually have a difficult time keeping a job.

Some people who have antisocial personality disorder are unable to feel remorse or guilt when they hurt other people. However, this should not be seen as a generalization because there are cases where people with antisocial personality disorder are still able to feel remorse about a situation.

Around 23% of people with borderline personality disorder also have ASPD. For a long time, it was thought that antisocial personality disorder was untreatable. Recent studies have shown that cognitive behavioral therapy has been the most effective in addressing the symptoms of ASPD. Other forms of treatment such as family-based and psychodynamic treatment are also beneficial in treating ASPD.

7. **Histrionic Personality Disorder:** Also known as HPD, this disorder is characterized by excessive attention-seeking and emotionality. Symptoms of histrionic personality disorder are usually manifested in early adulthood. Other symptoms of HPD include:

- Feeling uncomfortable in situations where one is not the center of attention
- Interaction with other people that often leads to provocative or inappropriate sexual behavior
- The use of physical appearance to draw attention to oneself
- Uses theatrical words and dramatics to express emotions
- Easily influenced by circumstances and other people

- Perceives relationships to be more intimate than they really are

People who have histrionic personality disorder are generally found to be emotional, dramatic, and lacking in attention. It can be elevated to a clinical disorder when it interferes with one's work and personal relationships.

Individuals with BPD and HPD have rapidly changing emotions and also have tendencies to be impulsive.

8. **Post-Traumatic Stress Disorder:** Also referred to as PTSD, post-traumatic stress disorder and borderline personality disorder are commonly co-occurring disorders because both of them are caused by traumatic events. The same behaviors, thoughts, and feelings manifested by BPD are also seen in those who suffer from PTSD. Additionally, the impulsive behavior as well as unstable relationships that dominate the lives of people with borderline personality disorder place them at greater risk for experiencing traumatic situations such as physical or sexual assault or getting into vehicle accidents.

9. **Dependent Personality Disorder:** Also known as DPD, dependent personality disorder is defined as an extreme need to be taken care of. DPD is also a common co-occurring disorder

found in people who have borderline personality disorder.

People with DPD are described to be very clingy and have difficulties making decisions without consulting the help of other people. Without the presence or advise of others, they tend to feel alone and helpless. It is common for people who have DPD to have unstable relationships as well because they have a constant need for support and validation. There is a significant overlap in the symptoms of both DPD and BPD, primarily the fear of perceived rejection. Those who have dependent personality disorder treat rejection and criticism the same way that borderlines do. Due to the overlap, treatment that is effective for BPD such as Dialectical Behavior Therapy will also work in reducing symptoms of DPD.

Chapter 4: How Borderline Personality Disorder Affects Families

Just like any disorder, a mental illness in the family would affect the entire unit as a whole. It has an acute effect on those with personality disorders because it affects interpersonal relationships. The impact of BPD is most felt on the families of those with the illness, an effect that also bounces back on the individual who is suffering.

Families of people with borderline personality disorder are affected in various ways. One or two people are usually designated as the case manager for their family member. It is also common to observe gender stereotyping because the women in the family, by default, are given the responsibility to take care of a family member who is sick; personality disorders included. Studies have also shown that family members of people who suffer from a mental disorder are more prone to becoming depressed. A relative with mental illness such as borderline personality disorder often has feelings of isolation and grief. Naturally, this would also result in feeling emotionally overburdened. In fact, research shows that suicide attempts and patient anger are leading causes of stress for mental health providers. These depressive symptoms are also evident in borderline personality disorder, further proving that the illness remains to have a significant effect on families and loved ones.

Family members also tend to feel overwhelmed in managing the symptoms of a relative with BPD. Additionally, they don't have the training, skills, and experience to manage it effectively while living normal lives of their own. Borderline personality disorder has a strong impact on families, and this fact should not be overlooked. Family members may end up feeling traumatized and this will make them emotionally incapable of taking care of their relative and providing any form of moral support. Statistics show that 10% of individuals with borderline personality disorder commit suicide, placing emphasis on the importance of care a person receives.

However, studies show that when family members are more emotionally engaged with their ill relative, the patient significantly improves their chances of reducing symptoms over the course of a year.

Although limited, there are therapeutic options that family members of those with borderline personality disorder can try. The primary reason behind this is that there the research on family relationships of those with BPD and other mental illnesses remains inadequate today. But given that the statistics estimate around 2 percent of the population are diagnosed with borderline personality disorder, this means that millions of family members are affected. When family members participate in counseling and programs that are designed for their own well-being, this will greatly benefit all parties involved.

Current programs that are aimed at providing support towards family members are derived from Dialectical Behavior Therapy as well as the stress coping and adaptation model. These have proven effective and should be a serious consideration for anyone who has a loved one suffering from borderline personality disorder. The stress coping and adaptation model focuses on healing based on a person's adaptive abilities, resources, and individual strengths. This leads to adaptive coping as it helps strengthen a person's way of dealing with the issue by applying both behavioral and cognitive techniques.

Dialectical behavior therapy is one of the more popular and effective methods of treating borderline personality disorder and its symptoms. This form of therapy is highly recommended for family members of those who have BPD because it focuses on change, coping strategies, and acceptance. The most effective treatment for borderline personality disorder combines teaching communication skills and coping strategies for the patient while also providing support through group networks for the family members.

Dealing with Siblings who have BPD

Sibling relationship can be multifaceted and complex at times. Usually, jealousy and competitiveness are present especially in the desire to seek approval from parents. If a sibling is diagnosed with borderline personality disorder, this may result in intense negative emotional experiences between siblings.

Children and teenagers who have BPD normally are at the receiving end of most of the attention at home. If you have a brother whose emotional behavior demanded that your parents focus more on him, this may cause you to feel resentment, jealousy, and neglect. The burden of witnessing negative behavior and the stress that your sibling's BPD symptoms has on the family also falls on you. However, when your sibling takes action to seek out treatment for BPD, it is crucial that they feel the support of the entire family including you. Working through your own feelings will be an important catalyst in changing the family dynamic, helping you and your sibling move forward for the benefit of the family unit as a whole.

Feeling angry, resentful, and jealous is normal before a sibling is treated for BPD. However, it is recognized that individuals who suffer as a result of a sibling's BPD symptoms have needs that need to be addressed too. While people with BPD need full emotional and moral support from their loved ones, their families are in need of the same things as well. Support groups focused on families of those who have BPD are an excellent place to start and will help you learn more about the disorder. Support groups will also help you work through the complex feelings you are experiencing as a result of being the affected sibling of someone who is borderline.

When facing this challenge, remember that you are not alone because many other brothers and sisters have had to deal with the trauma of growing up with a sibling who suffered from BPD. Support groups provide helpful validation of the experience as a whole and can help you see things in a new perspective. Furthermore, support groups can also teach you about effective communication techniques that you can apply when talking to a sibling who has BPD.

By educating yourself about the disorder, you can identify skills that will prove indispensable in dealing family members with BPD. More importantly you will learn how to best support your sibling at a time when they need you the most, even though they don't act like it. You will also learn to set boundaries as you empower yourself so that you will no longer feel like you are at the receiving end of your sibling's negative emotional outbursts.

Once your sibling begins treatment for borderline personality disorder, they are clearly communicating that they have invested in improving their interpersonal relationships. However, the road to recovery may be full of obstacles and oftentimes won't be easy for them. They may show signs of improvement but with certain stressors may end up taking a step back to destructive behavior. It is up to the family, siblings involved, to help them through the journey as they full recover from BPD. Providing moral support to someone who has BPD also means taking care of yourself emotionally and physically in order to give the best possible support you can.

It is also important to remember that a sibling who has BPD will not have it for life. Borderline personality disorder is a curable disorder, but the earlier it is diagnosed the more effective and successful treatment will be. Since BPD is often characterized by feelings of abandonment, depression, and feeling highly emotional, your sibling will appreciate working through the ordeal with them. Once it's all over you can expect to have a more fulfilling relationship with them.

Mothers With Borderline Personality Disorder and Its Effect on Childhood Development

Childhood is a time where both parents and child learn new things and face challenges. For the child, it is when they are most sensitive to their environment. It is when they are more vulnerable to anything that may affect their development. If a mother has borderline personality disorder, it can create an added battle to the existing trials of growing up.

The National Institute of Health states that mothers with BPD symptoms are considered high-risk caregivers because of the many psychological characteristics that usually lead to negative outcomes in their own children. People with borderline personality disorder commonly have stormy and intense relationships, and mother-child relationships are no different. Mothers may have difficulty controlling their impulses and end up being angry at their child, and may even exhibit suicidal behavior. If a child witnesses BPD symptoms in their mother, who is their primary caregiver, it reduces the opportunity for the mother and child to develop stable environments that are necessary for them to develop healthy attachments to one another. Each child will have their own ups and downs in life, in the same way that there is no such thing as the perfect mother regardless of BPD.

Mothers who suffer from borderline personality disorder should participate in treatment so that they can give their children a better chance to experience stability and security. It is their responsibility to work on getting better so that they can lay out the foundation for developing better relationships with their child. When mothers do this, they also do something that is very important: preventing borderline personality disorder from being passed down to the next generation.

It is also helpful for mothers who have BPD to be educated about child rearing. They can learn additional strategies in child development while coping with the illness. Mindfulness based strategies are ideal so they can continue to be a source of warmth while monitoring their child.

Dialectical Behavior Therapy provides mothers with the emotional awareness and mindfulness skills that they need to be more effective at child rearing. Mothers who have BPD should seek help in treatment centers who have a strong focus on Dialectical Behavior Therapy so they can recover from their symptoms.

Dealing with Parents Who Have Borderline Personality Disorder

If one of your parents has BPD, you may have had a challenging upbringing. When a parent has BPD it may oftentimes have a negative effect on their children although this is not always the case. Unfortunately, it can have a serious impact on the emotions and psychological health of their child.

Children of parents who have borderline personality disorder don't have a sense of boundaries, suffer from low self-esteem, and have shame and anger issues that go on for a long time unless addressed properly. A parent who has BPD may have neglected their child's emotional, physical, or psychological needs. In extreme cases, all three of these aspects could be completely neglected. Children of those with BPD can benefit greatly from support groups designed primarily for them.

Starting the discussion with someone who has borderline personality disorder because you want them to seek help can have either positive or negative outcomes. Due to their sensitivity this kind of conversation can result in an emotional outburst. Within families, this may result in conflict and distance. People with BPD already feel that they are always being attacked, and confronting them about a mental illness could end up disastrous. The conversation will make a big difference, and should be well-thought about to reduce the chances of it going badly.

However, a parent who has never sought treatment for borderline personality disorder or who denied a diagnosis in the past may pose an added challenge. In fact they may even accuse you as the one who is mentally ill. They may put blame for many problems encountered in your own relationship. If this happens, it is best that you focus on your own healing rather than expecting the other person to change.

How to Cope With A Mother Who Has BPD

If you have a mother who has borderline personality disorder, you are most likely experiencing a difficult relationship with them. Mothers with BPD can behave erratically, ranging from insisting on being over-involved in their children's lives, or neglecting them completely.

Although your mother may not have been diagnosed with BPD, here are some symptoms that you should watch out for:

- **Over-control:** A common characteristic of parents with borderline personality disorder is the urge to control their children's actions, feelings, and behaviors. At times the desire to control becomes an obstacle to their child's growth and ability to develop.

- **Neglect:** Mothers with BPD may oftentimes be so absorbed in their seemingly overwhelming emotions that they end up neglecting their children. Sometimes it is so severe that they are completely unable to put their child's needs before theirs.

- **Criticism:** Mothers with BPD are known to consistently insult or discourage their children, instead of showing them love and nurturing such as a normal mother would do. BPD mothers usually see their children as their extension, which results in the parent projecting negative feelings because it is what they see in themselves.

- **Blame:** Borderline mothers tend to put the blame for their sadness, anger, and frustration on their children. People with BPD have a difficult time being accountable for their actions and emotions.

Children who are raised by borderline mothers can develop numerous emotional issues as they grow older. They find it more difficult to overcome the hurtful past experienced with the BPD parent and oftentimes need to seek professional help in moving on.

If you are a child of a mother with BPD, you may experience low self-esteem, depression, or anger. The first step towards healing is to recognize that your mother's behavior is not your fault. In order to move forward it is also ideal to talk to family, friends, support groups, and even therapists who can provide moral support. Releasing your feelings in safe places will allow you to validate your own emotions and get rid of pain. There are also many ways you can change the dynamic of your relationship with your mother. It is possible to learn how to create boundaries and help yourself reduce feelings of obligation as well as guilt.

Does BPD Run in the Family?

Many parents with borderline personality disorder worry about passing it on to their children. While it is possible that your children may develop BPD later in life, it is not a guarantee because many BPD parents can learn how to raise their children and allow them to live a healthy life without inheriting the illness.

Some studies show that borderline personality disorder can run in families but there are many factors that contribute to this. Because genetics is a suspected cause of BPD, there is a small chance that your biological children can inherit certain genes from you making them more vulnerable to developing BPD.

More importantly, the kind of environment your child lives in has a greater impact in determining if they will develop borderline personality disorder. For example, if your BPD symptoms cause you to harm your child, this makes them more prone to it because they have been caused harm and possibly trauma. It can be challenging to be an effective parent if you have BPD.

While nothing can be done about genetics, parents with BPD have more control about ensuring that their children have a healthy, happy home to reduce the environmental factors that contribute to the disorder. The kind of environment a child lives in can influence the occurrence of BPD more than any other known factor.

If you are a parent with borderline personality disorder, the most important task you need to do is to ensure you are getting proper treatment. Being under the guidance of a mental health professional or therapist can greatly improve your condition which will benefit your parenting skills as well. In fact, after the first round of treatment many people are no longer considered diagnosed with borderline personality disorder. When you have less symptoms to deal with you will be able to focus on becoming a better parent.

During the course of your treatment, you should be open about asking questions to your therapist. They may be able to assist in evaluating the current home environment, and assess if your parenting skills are affected by BPD. They could also provide you with better resources such as referring you to a program that provides training and coping mechanisms for parents dealing with BPD. Depending on the severity of the illness, some parents with BPD can still turn out to be nurturing and effective although for others it takes some time.

How To Help Your Child Deal With BPD in College

Borderline personality disorder results in highly unstable emotions which can be an obstacle at being successful in school. Managing the symptoms of BPD is crucial so that your child can reach their educational goals. As a parent there are things you can do to help your child cope with BPD and even support them in attaining one or more degrees.

Talk to your child about learning how to cope with stress whenever possible. College and university life can be a high-stress environment where seemingly simple things such as waking up early each day to go to class, making the time to study, and performing exceptionally well can place a strain on children with BPD. Living with BPD also means that one has a more difficult time dealing with stress as compared to their peers. While other schoolmates may perceive stress as a normal part of life in higher education, your child may be overwhelmed simply because they have BPD.

Although the stressors cannot be changed, you can help your child manage them better. Be supportive if they prefer to take on a smaller work load per semester, take online courses, or be a nontraditional student so that they can focus on work with less stress each day. Emphasize the importance of getting adequate sleep and proper nutrition which will be important sources of energy especially with all the studying that they need to do. Your child may also benefit from healthy social connections found in school groups as well as their own family and friends, so you can encourage them to make friends that will aid in alleviating the burden of higher education.

While most children see going away to college as the norm, a child with BPD may feel comfortable studying in a location that is closer to home. Be supportive if they feel this way because their home support system is crucial to them. If your child feels lonely this can worsen the symptoms of BPD by provoking fear of abandonment and other symptoms.

How To Help Your Loved One Start Their Career

Many kids will soon face graduation and along with that comes some daunting questions about major life decisions. If your child is one of them and is suffering from borderline personality disorder, your support will be crucial to their success in the real world.

While these major life decisions can be challenging to anyone, people with BPD may face this with more fear and anxiety than others. This is because they need to be strong in the event of being rejected from a job they have been wanting, be more determined and focused, and make new friends at their new jobs. Remember that individuals with borderline personality disorder already suffer from these symptoms:

- Intense fear of rejection
- Disturbed sense of identity
- Anxiety
- Impulsivity
- Difficulty maintaining stable relationships

Not everyone who has borderline personality disorder will struggle with starting their career. But for others the challenge can be life-long and oftentimes paralyzing. As parents, you have to be realistic in helping your child succeed. Discuss career goals with children but keep in mind that it takes time, so it is best to avoid putting too much pressure on them because they are dealing with BPD. Since they tend to see everything in black and white they also usually have an all or nothing attitude towards events, people, and situations. If a job interview did not go well they may end up convincing themselves that they made the wrong decision or that they may never find a job at all. Help them realize that there are steps to succeeding and that one rejection doesn't mean they will fail.

Help your child concentrate on making small steps towards reaching their goals. If they focus on only one major goal this can be frustrating and will cause them to give up. Have them focus on small accomplishments that will not only help them move forward but that will also help them to feel good. Encourage them to focus their efforts on sending out at least 5 job applications a day to better improve their chances at landing a job. When they do accomplish these goals, celebrate with them. The moral support lent by parents, family, and friends mean the world to people with borderline personality disorder.

It is also important for parents to keep their cool regardless of the outcome of a job interview. Whether it is positive or negative, be supportive of your child. Recognize their success and also empathize with them if they are dealing with failure or rejection. When talking to your child about the outcome of a job interview or their first day at work, use an even tone of voice that will ensure your support and care for them regardless of their performance at the job. If they find that the learning curve is difficult, provide concrete ways of helping them learn what they need to do in order to work better. For example, they may feel completely in the dark about how to create professional emails and proposals. Sit down with them and teach them how to write emails but encourage them to be independent in seeking resources and information that will help them learn.

Encourage them to keep a routine which will help them stay sane despite what feels like crazy days when one is in the midst of building their career. By having a strong, healthy routine in place it will give them more control. Help them create a routine that works for them, such as certain times of the day that are dedicated to job searches, sending out applications, and making phone calls. It is just as important to ensure that they have a time in the day that they can step away from the job hunt and instead focus on themselves, engaging in activities that make them feel good such as spending time with friends or participating in their favorite hobby.

When young people with borderline personality disorder are just starting out their career, the support of family and friends can make the difference from success and failure. If the symptoms of BPD make it difficult for them to starting or keeping a job, treatment is needed.

Once the symptoms are under control they can start their career on the right foot. In fact, many borderline personality disorder treatment centers also offer vocational assistance which can also help your loved one in creating a resume, starting the job hunt, and coaching for interviews.

Borderline Personality Disorder in Children and Adolescents

It may be difficult to diagnose borderline personality disorder in children because the symptoms they exhibit can develop into other disorders as they grow. However, parents may still observe indications of BPD in children before the illness develops further. Some parents have reported observing symptoms of borderline personality disorder in their children even if they are just a year old. Infants who display BPD tend to cry more, have difficulty sleeping, are affected by changes in their routine, and are more challenging to soothe when crying or upset.

Toddlers who are diagnosed with borderline personality disorder tend to be more demanding. If they have siblings, they usually require more attention and reassurance from their parents. They also tend to experience bouts of sadness, worry more, are more sensitive, and easily become upset. When children with BPD experience frustrations, it is met with tantrum episodes which oftentimes can be on the severe side. They may also experience separation anxiety when leaving their homes to attend school. If under stress, they may resort to pulling hair or suffer from stomach cramps, inability to rest well, or have headaches. These are all because children with BPD simply do not know how to adapt to stressful situations. Parents of children with borderline personality disorder are often called to the school to discuss problematic behavior with teachers and counselors. It is also common for them to be the "problem child" in school, the child whose emotions are too intense to handle while other children their age seem to be coping just fine.

Today, there is little known about how adults with BPD behaved when they were children. Although there is insufficient medical literature detailing the characteristics of children with BPD, it is still possible to diagnose them early on because of their intense emotions and impulsivity. The characteristics mentioned above describe the behavior of children who are usually diagnosed with mental health illnesses later in life, such as borderline personality disorder.

The Link Between Childhood Bullying and Borderline Personality Disorder

Childhood bullying can seriously harm a child both emotionally and physically. It can be so damaging that it will result in a lifelong trauma to the affected child. Studies have shown that childhood bullying can actually make one more vulnerable to developing borderline personality disorder.

Other factors will also increase a child's risk for developing BPD. These include sexual abuse and hostility from parents. Chronic childhood bullying that occurs anywhere until a child has become a teenager, can increase one's risk for developing BPD by as much as five times. If your child is being bullied at school, it may be time to coordinate with the school and find out how you can improve the situation.

Parenting Techniques for Children with BPD

If you have a child who has borderline personality disorder, there are additional parenting challenges. At times it may feel like the very task of parenting is overwhelming, causing stress and tension in the household. A child who manifests compulsive behavior and is constantly angry and depressive can turn a household upside down, but educating yourself about the validating techniques for raising a child with BPD can restore your home back into a peaceful, harmonious one.

Children as well as young adults who suffer from borderline personality disorder are vulnerable to emotional instability and low-self-esteem. They often feel that they are not understood, and that they are disliked by friends and family. As a response to this they may resort to erratic behavior but parents can help address these negative emotions, reducing the stress that their children are experiencing. Parents can also be instrumental in helping their children manage BPD symptoms more effectively.

Validating techniques include the following:

1. Always approach your children with warmth especially when engaging them in conversation. The relationship you have with your child may be strained due to emotional conflict and behavior that leaves you feeling frustrated as a parent. However, you can take action to resolve these issues by approaching them with warmth and becoming interested in their lives.

2. The most important way you can validate your child's emotions is by giving them your full attention when they speak. Make it a point to really listen, and look them in the eye to show that you are paying attention to every word. Echo what they tell you to prove that you listened, and avoid negative statements such as telling them they should not be feeling a certain way. The point here is to allow your child to recognize that their feelings are valid rather than dismissing their emotions by telling them what they should and shouldn't be feeling.

3. Show your child your human side and be yourself. Remember that you don't always have to conform to the role of a strict parent or disciplinarian because sometimes all it takes is showing your child a natural side of you. By doing this you are encouraging a relationship between you and your child that connects you both on a different level.

4. If your child has difficulty expressing themselves, try to help them articulate their feelings. This will help your child feel that you understand them, and this will lead to validation, allowing them to move forward from their negative emotions.

5. Be your child's biggest cheerleader to show that you have full confidence in their ability to succeed in life. Whenever they do well in school, be generous with praise and reinforce positive behavior.

What To Do If Your Child Refuses BPD Treatment

If you have a child who has borderline personality disorder, you may encounter difficulties getting them to avail of treatment. This can happen regardless if your child is in their 20's or is a toddler. Treatment will be crucial to their development as a mature individual but not all children are willing.

The first step you can do to get them to seek treatment is to educate them about borderline personality disorder. They may not understand what BPD is all about and the benefits that treatment can do for them and their future. Open the space for dialogue about it, and encourage them to ask all the questions they may have. When your child is powered with knowledge and confident that treatment will help them, they may feel more empowered to accept treatment.

It is also necessary for parents to keep in mind that a child with BPD will often feel misunderstood, resulting in mood swings, unstable relationships, and compulsive behavior. Your child will go through most days feeling unaccepted, lonely, and unheard even by those that they love. In order to convince your child to accept treatment, parents should be empathetic towards them and show them that you understand what they are going through. You can express this by letting them know why they act a certain way sometimes. Once your child feels that they are understood, they are more likely to accept treatment for BPD.

In the event that your child does not understand what BPD treatment will entail, invest the time in educating them about it. You may even take them to a therapist or BPD treatment center specializing in children with BPD. Professionals may help communicate how treatment works, and what will be expected of the child. Older children such as adolescents and those in their 20's could benefit from talking to support groups and people who are on the road to recovery from BPD. This kind of interaction can greatly change the way your child perceives the disorder and treatment.

In some instances, tough love is required especially if your child completely refuses to be treated regardless of what you do. Tough love may take the form of denying them financial assistance or withdrawing their allowance. While this may sound manipulative, sometime tough love is the only way you can get your child to agree to treatment. If you decide that tough love is the way to go because all other methods have failed, try to be as balanced as you can by being empathic and showing love but telling them that they will be denied certain comforts until they complete treatment.

The reward system may also be advantageous in convincing your child to get help. For example if your child has been asking for theater lessons, you can use this as a reward for them once they complete therapy. Your older child may have been wanting to move out to their own apartment, to which you could use financial assistance as reward once they complete the course of treatment.

Parents should not give up on ensuring their children receive adequate treatment for borderline personality disorder, otherwise symptoms could exacerbate with age and worse, your child may resort to self-harm.

Chapter5: Borderline Personality Disorder in the Workplace

Employees with personality disorders may have an impact on the entire workplace. An employee with mental illness may be difficult to manage and work with. They may resort to physical aggression, threatening, and harassment, severely damaging their jobs and those that they work with.

The Journal of Business and Economics Research published a study which revealed that borderline personality disorder is among the top traits found in difficult employees and managers. However, when BPD and its associated characteristics are better understood, this helps managers and coworkers manage an employee more effectively.

People with borderline personality disorder can have disruptive effects in the workplace. If a working individual isn't managing his symptoms, their intense emotions and impulsiveness will eventually lead to dissatisfaction among other employees. But if managers make sure that they have a healthy working environment to begin with, people with BPD may benefit from the stability. Stress experienced in the workplace can provoke the symptoms of BPD, affecting everyone involved.

Those suffering from borderline personality disorder may have feelings of rejection or abandonment which will result in divisiveness wherever they go. They may also experience suppressed feelings of anger that will cause them to devaluate people in their workplace. It is a natural tendency of people with BPD to categorize people in their lives as either good or bad, and they will do the same in their work environment. This kind of personality leads to unstable professional relationships. It may be manifested by the use of manipulation and empathy to make a coworker feel used. Many employees with borderline personality disorder spread gossip so that coworkers are divided amongst each other. They also tend to unload personal drama and stress on other people. Employees may also feel insecure when around a coworker with borderline personality disorder. All of these can cause productivity to suffer. However, a positive effect of working with someone with BPD is that their divisiveness makes them more competitive because they have an innate desire to be recognized.

For management, it may be challenging interacting with their employees who have borderline personality disorder. Although it is difficult to detect the symptoms, management can work on creating a harmonious workplace by placing a strong emphasis on a healthy work environment. It would also be ideal to have feedback mechanisms in place with repercussions involved, detailed all in the employee handbook. This would communicate to all employees that management takes employee well-being seriously, and that there are consequences for those who break the rules. Management is responsible for setting limitations on conduct, ensuring focus on assigned tasks, and making it clear that consideration of coworker's feelings is important.

People with borderline personality disorder have a history of numerous job changes because they are unable to cope with the stress and may have been unable to develop healthy working relationships with people in the office. But it is important for management to recognize that they play a role in managing their employees, even those with a personality disorder. It is not impossible to have a successful business even if an employee has BPD.

Any kind of criticism at work can inflame symptoms of BPD such as abandonment fears. Individuals with borderline personality disorder already feel emotions more intensely than others and this will cause them to be angry at their supervisors. They may resort to self-injury and have heated outbursts. Managers and supervisors should be prepared for possible angry protests, or that an employee with BPD will be angry towards you for reasons unknown.

Employees with personality disorders can affect the work environment and productivity as a whole. This is why it is necessary for managers to address issues as early as possible. Any problems that arise should be dealt with directly and they should be able to provide alternatives in order to come up with a solution. It should also be remembered that because people with borderline personality disorder already experience instability in their lives, it would be helpful for managers to promote consistency wherever possible in the workplace. Most importantly, being informed about the challenges of living with borderline personality disorder will greatly help manage the situation more efficiently because when someone with BPD is employed in your business, there is a strong need to educate everyone involved. Management should invest time in learning about the condition thoroughly so that they can deal with it when situations arise in the workplace. All employees will also benefit from learning about borderline personality disorder, including its causes, symptoms, and treatment options so that they can understand the affected employee better and show compassion. Even people with BPD can benefit from being educated about it especially if they have not been diagnosed or are not receiving treatment.

If all else fails, managers can also convince the employee with BPD to talk to someone in the Employee Assistance Program at the company. Let them know that doing so can help them get over a difficult period or learn how to deal with stress better. Although most people think that if someone tried hard enough, they can control mood swings and behave better. But for those with borderline personality disorder this is not always the case. Those with BPD may sometimes need professional treatment so that their behavior doesn't interfere with their professional life. If an employee decides to seek help, be supportive and give them a positive attitude. You may be investing in an employee whose improvement will make them valuable to the company in the future.

Chapter 6: Diagnosis

Borderline personality disorder is often misdiagnosed or under diagnosed. Thorough interviews and detailed discussions about symptoms will help medical professionals diagnose BPD more efficiently. Symptoms of BPD are similar to other mental disorders and co-occurring illnesses, which is also why a thorough discussion and investigation of symptoms is required for proper diagnosis.

During the discussion, medical professionals typically inquire about family medical history, personal medical history, history of mental illness, and the symptoms being experienced. This kind of information will help determine the best course of treatment for the individual if indeed they are found to have borderline personality disorder. Additionally, this information will rule out other mental illnesses. An individual must also meet the criteria defined by Diagnostic and Statistical Manual of Mental Disorders (DSM). Incorrect diagnosis may occur if a person describes being depressed without revealing other symptoms they are experiencing.

A thorough investigation is necessary to diagnose borderline personality disorder because there is no single test that can determine if a person has the illness or not. At least 5 of the characteristics below should be present for one to be diagnosed with BPD:

- Unstable relationships
- Self-harm
- Chronically feeling empty
- Impulsive behavior
- Fear of abandonment
- Paranoia
- Losing contact with reality
- Chronic mood swings
- Anger management issues

Adults with borderline personality disorder are usually those who are diagnosed. Children or teenagers tend to exhibit symptoms that closely resembled BPD which eventually go away as they get older and mature.

3 Reasons Why BPD Is Misdiagnosed

Borderline personality disorder is a common disorder that affects 2% of the population. People with BPD tend to have emotional outbursts, unstable relationships, a distorted self-image, and unpredictable mood swings among other symptoms.

BPD is commonly misdiagnosed for many reasons. One of the reasons is that its symptoms closely resemble those of Bipolar Disorder. Other reasons why it is usually misdiagnosed include:

1. BPD appears with the presence of co-occurring disorders. Borderline people often also suffer from depression, anxiety, and eating disorders. This may result in doctors failing to isolate symptoms of BPD especially because these symptoms are also present in numerous other psychological illnesses.

2. The symptoms of BPD often aren't manifested early on. Some behavioral characteristics may be seen as normal in the beginning. However, symptoms can worsen as a person stays in a longer relationship with someone who has BPD. It is usually when people with BPD begin to develop a dependency on their partner that the symptoms begin to show more clearly.

3. The diagnostic criteria for BPD is oftentimes confusing. A person who is aggressive and difficult may be over diagnosed for having borderline personality disorder when in reality they are not mentally ill. They may simply be acting out that way because someone else provokes that kind of attitude in them.

Because of the confusing diagnostic criteria for BPD, it may be difficult for therapists to get the diagnosis correct all on the first try. The best way to save time and money on your diagnosis is by going to a medical professional who has years of experience in borderline personality disorder. It is never recommended to do a self-diagnosis of BPD but it is always good to be aware of the symptoms so that you would know if it's necessary to check for a diagnosis.

Avoiding Self-Diagnosis

With the widespread dependence on the internet as a reference for virtually anything under the sun, it can be tempting to avoid going to a doctor and resorting to the internet. It is common for people to go online as soon as they experience any symptoms in order to get answers for what they are experiencing. Self-diagnosis is never recommended and can be particularly harmful for those who are actually suffering from borderline personality disorder.

One of the primary reasons why self-diagnosis is a bad idea is that you can miss out on co-occurring disorders. For example those who suffer from panic disorders may completely miss out on being diagnosed for irregular heartbeats as a result of panic. In more serious cases, brain tumors are responsible for depression, changes in personality, and psychotic episodes. While some people feel that it is acceptable to miss treatment for psychological illnesses and deal with it, this should not be the case for something as fatal as brain tumors.

Self-diagnosis should also be avoided because it is impossible to be objective about your own symptoms. If you suspect that you have borderline personality disorder or any other psychological illness for that matter, it is always best to leave it in the hands of a professional. A trained medical doctor has the skills and expertise in providing you with an objective diagnosis, and guide you to recovery when needed.

Each time you attempt to self-diagnose, you have a high risk of resulting in a wrong diagnosis. This may lead you to seek treatment for an incorrect diagnosis or even worse resorting to self-help remedies that are not made for the condition you may have. When it comes to borderline personality disorder you always want to be sure of what you are getting yourself into. In fact you may not have BPD at all, and are merely over diagnosing yourself when you are stressed or under extreme pressure.

Chapter 7: Treatment and Medication

Each person's experience with borderline personality disorder is different. Some symptoms may be more dominant; while for one he could be more paranoid, for another he would be more dissociative. Depending on the situation and circumstances, a therapist can recommend the right treatment for borderline personality disorder.

In addition, it may be tempting for some people with BPD to attempt managing the disorder without resorting to therapy. In order to fully recover from the symptoms, one must be able to learn coping skills that they need to manage BPD every day. The urge to manage BPD without professional therapeutic help may have stemmed from negative experiences with doctors and therapists in the past. But without the commitment to recover fully from borderline personality disorder, the chances of overcoming the symptoms are highly unlikely without the guidance of therapy.

Therapy teaches important life skills that are needed by people who suffer from BPD, if they want to enjoy living a normal life again. These life skills are also crucial if the patient wants to enjoy a quality life. There are many resources on how one can self-help to reduce symptoms of

BPD, but without the guidance of a licensed professional who is dedicated to helping you manage your disorder, you will never have an objective understanding or know if you have actually recovered from your illness.

The recovery process can be difficult alone, which is why this book discusses how family, friends, and loved ones can provide actual support. The moral support lent by loved ones will be valuable in recovery. Additionally, because borderline personality disorder is an actual mental condition, it is not advisable to go about it without professional intervention. If BPD is left untreated it can lead to serious consequences on oneself and to loved ones.

When one has BPD it can oftentimes be a scary experience that leaves one feeling isolated because it causes a strain on relationships. Individuals with BPD need the guidance of therapists to overcome this aspect of the disorder so that they can go back to their normal life and benefit from the joy that healthy human relationships can bring. Treatment for BPD can provide people with valuable skills that they need to carry out into the world for maintaining interpersonal relationships. Additionally, treatment can reduce the stress involved through the prescription of medication that decreases BPD symptoms.

Psychotherapy

Psychotherapy is the most common treatment of choice for people with mental illnesses especially those who have BPD. Although there are many forms of psychotherapy, they all have one goal in common and that is to help patients better understand the way their thoughts and emotions operate. It is an important aspect of treatment because while medication can help reduce certain symptoms of borderline personality disorder, it will not teach patients how to learn coping skills or regulate emotions the way psychotherapy does.

Psychotherapy is also crucial in helping people refrain from committing suicide. This is why therapists and other medical professionals involved stay in touch with the patient, constantly evaluating their vulnerability to suicide throughout the entire treatment. When a patient has severe feelings of suicide, hospitalization is the next step.

Dialectical Behavior Therapy

The most famous and effective form of psychotherapy known today is Dialectical Behavior Therapy or DBT. It was founded by Marsha Linehan, and is a program that teaches people how to take better control of their lives and emotions. DBT also has a strong focus on emotion regulation, self-knowledge, and cognitive restructuring. DBT has a comprehensive approach and is usually conducted with a group. However, the skill set taught through Dialectical Behavior Therapy is considered complex and therefore not recommended to people who have difficulty learning new concepts.

Dialectical Behavior Therapy utilizes two concepts: validation and dialectics. In validation, the client is taught to accept that their emotions are real, acceptable, and valid. On the other hand, dialectics is a form of philosophy which teaches that life is not to be seen as black and white. It also reinforces the importance of accepting ideas even though they are contradicting to one's own beliefs.

The primary goal of DBT is to help the client break their notions of the world and enjoy freedom from living a rigid life that causes one to resort to self-destructive behavior. DBT is held in weekly group as well as individual sessions. Clients are given a number that they can call any time if they feel that their symptoms are getting worse and need emergency assistance. In order for DBT to be effective, teamwork is expected. Clients need to work closely with their therapists as well as the other people met during group sessions.

While Dialectical Behavior Therapy is generally the most successful form of treating BPD, it has shown to be particularly useful in treating those who are more prone to suicide. Individuals with

BPD resort to suicide because they feel that they have lost absolutely all control in life and suicide is the only thing they can do that can help them. Dialectical Behavior Therapy is particularly effective in helping people regain a sense of control in their lives. Once DBT has helped a patient be in control, therapists can focus on other aspects of their life to improve.

Therapists specializing in DBT work with those who are prone to suicide by engaging them in mindfulness, interpersonal effectiveness, emotion regulation, and distress tolerance. When people with BPD learn that there are healthy ways of coping and handling one's emotions, the risk of them committing self-harm and suicide are significantly decreased.

Borderline personality disorder, just like other personality disorders, is challenging to treat. Because the goal of treatment is to change the way a person views the world, stress, and other people, treatment is usually lengthy. Treatment for BPD is usually at least a year but can go on for much longer.

There are also other forms of psychotherapy that are used to address borderline personality disorder that focus on conflict resolution and social learning theory. These are more solution-focused therapies which fail to address the core issue of people who suffer from BPD which is difficulty regulating their emotions.

Schema Focused Therapy

Schema Focused Therapy is a type of psychotherapy whose primary goal is to identify and treat unhealthy ways of thinking. Some elements of schema focused therapy include elements that are also found in cognitive behavioral therapy (CBT) and combines it with other methods of psychotherapy.

Schema focused therapy is founded on the principle that if a person's basic childhood needs such as love, acceptance, and a desire for safety are inadequate, this results in the development of unhealthy ways of thinking about the world. These are referred to as maladaptive early schemas. Schemes are defined as broad patterns of behavior and thinking. They are more than simply beliefs because they are closely held patterns that affect the way one perceives and interacts with the world.

The schema theory suggests that schemas occur when events in one's present life bear a resemblance to events in the past that are directly related to the creation of the schema. When a person has unhealthy schemas as a result of a difficult childhood, they will end up developing unhealthy ways of thinking as a response to the situation. Furthermore, schema theory suggests that the symptoms of borderline personality disorder are usually caused by a difficult childhood wherein a child may have experienced abandonment, trauma, or maltreatment by one or both parents, resulting to the development of maladaptive early schemas.

Schema focused therapy for borderline personality disorder seeks to identify relevant schemas in a person's life, and tie them to schemas present in past events. A therapist works to help the patient process the emotional response that arise due to the schema. They then work on addressing unhealthy coping methods to help the patient respond to the scheme in a healthy manner. Schema focused therapy may involve exercises that are designed to halt unhealthy behavioral patterns, change the way one thinks, and encouraging the patient to vent out their anger.

Transference Focused Therapy

Transference Focused Therapy utilizes the patient-therapist relationship in order to improve how a person with borderline personality disorder sees the world. Transference is defined as the process wherein emotions are transferred from one person to the other. It is a key principle used in psychodynamic therapies where it is suggested that the way a client feels about persons that are important in their lives are transferred to his therapist. Through transference therapy, the therapist can clearly understand how the patient interacts with the people in his life in order to help them learn to effectively manage relationships. Eventually, the goal of transference focused therapy is to help patients enjoy having stable relationships again.

Therapists of transference focused therapy believe that symptoms of borderline personality disorder that arise from dysfunctional relationships one experienced during childhood continue in adulthood, thereby damaging the ability of these adults to have normal, healthy relationships. The interactions we have with our primary caregivers during childhood contributes to how we develop a sense of self and also affects how we perceive other people. If one does not have a healthy relationship with their caregivers during childhood, this results in adults having difficulty relating to other people and having a good sense of oneself.

Evidence shows that maltreatment or trauma or loss of caregivers during childhood increases one's risk in developing borderline personality disorder. And because these symptoms have a negative impact, preventing one from developing relationships with people later on, some experts on BPD agree that it is important to address this by helping people focus on improving relationships through transference focused therapy.

With this kind of therapy there is a focus on the relationship between the patient and the therapist. Unlike other forms of therapy where the therapist provides instructions on what the patient should do, transference focused therapy involves asking the client numerous questions during the discussion while they explore reactions. Furthermore, there is added emphasis on events that happen in the present moment instead of seeking out past experiences. For example, instead of spending time discussing issues with caregivers during one's childhood, the discussion is focused on how the client relates to their own therapist.

Therapists who practice transference based therapy are also skilled at remaining neutral, which is a reason why this kind of treatment is effective. They know not to give their opinion on their patient's reaction, and will also not be available outside session hours except for emergencies.

Mentalization-Based Therapy

Mentalization-based therapy (MBT) is another form of psychotherapy. MBT is based on the premise that people who have borderline personality disorder have difficulty thinking about their own thoughts. This means that people with BPD are unable to examine their own thoughts, beliefs, opinions, and if they are realistic and useful to them. An example of this is when individuals with BPD may have sudden urges to harm themselves and end up giving in without thinking about the consequences of their actions.

MBT is also important because it helps people realize that others have their own thoughts and beliefs, and your own interpretation of their mental states is not always correct. Additionally, it helps people realize that actions will have an impact on other people's mentality. The main goal of MBT is to help clients recognize their own as well as others' mental states. It also teaches people with BPD how to step back from their own thoughts and examine if they are valid first. MBT may be conducted within a hospital as a form of inpatient therapy. Treatment is composed of daily sessions with a therapist as well as group sessions.

MBT usually lasts around 18 months, but depending on the need some patients may be asked to be an inpatient for the entire duration of their treatment. Some hospitals and treatment facilities will allow patients to leave at specified times during the course of their treatment.

Therapeutic Communities

Therapeutic Communities (TC) is a form of psychotherapy wherein people with various psychological conditions interact in a structured environment. This kind of treatment is best suited for those who have issues dealing with emotions and who are suicidal. By teaching them the skills needed for healthy social interaction with a wide range of people, people with borderline personality disorder can better cope with their problems. TC therapy is usually residential and held in houses where clients stay 1-4 days a week.

Apart from individual and group sessions involved in TC, it also requires patients to participate in other activities designed to improve one's social skills and boost confidence. These activities include doing household chores, prepare and cook meals, play games, and participate in recreational activities. Therapeutic communities also involve all participants in regular community meetings where people with different psychological conditions meet in order to discuss issues and concerns within the community.

One of the unique features of the therapeutic community method of treatment is that it is run democratically. All members, including staff, can contribute their opinion on how TC's should be run. In fact, they can even vote if they think an individual should or shouldn't be admitted within the community. This means that even if one's therapist thinks that a therapeutic community is the best form of treatment for a case of borderline personality disorder, it doesn't mean that they will automatically be granted entry. Guidelines for acceptable behavior are defined in each TC because they set restrictions such as the prohibition of alcohol consumption, violence towards one self and other members of the community. Members who break the guidelines may be asked to leave the TC.

Although a therapeutic community is one of the widely accepted methods of treatment for people with borderline personality disorder, there is insufficient evidence to tell if a TC is effective for everyone. This is particularly the case for people with BPD who have difficulty following rules since TC's can be quite strict with guidelines.

Self-Care

Over the course of treatment, patients are usually given a telephone number that they can call if they think they are undergoing a severe crisis. It could occur when people with BPD are experiencing episodes of extreme symptoms and are more prone to self-harm and suicide. A number may be directed to the community mental health care practitioners, social workers, or other medical professionals. Depending on the area, a crisis resolution team service may also be available since they specialize in caring for people with serious mental health issues. Oftentimes these teams come to the rescue of individuals who may require hospitalization because of suicide attempts.

Those who suffer from borderline personality disorder usually find that merely talking to someone about what they are going through can help them get out of their crisis. Certain cases, although rare, may require medication such as tranquilizers to calm one's mood. Medications such as these are usually prescribed for 7 days to stabilize emotions.

Individuals with borderline personality disorder are encouraged to attend support groups for social support from those who are going through the same experience as they are. Support groups are useful in providing moral support through sharing common thoughts and feelings. Patients can also try coping skills and learn how to regulate their emotions with friends they make at these support groups. They have proven to be a crucial part of helping people with BPD expand their skill set while developing healthy social relationships and eventually reduce their symptoms in the long run.

If you are the one suffering from borderline personality disorder, you may also find it challenging to take better care of yourself. However, those who are diagnosed with BPD should make it a priority to take better care of themselves because the symptoms may be exacerbated when one neglects self-care.

The basics of self-care involve engaging in activities that promote relaxation and good health. This means getting enough exercise, good sleep, taking the medications as prescribed by your therapist, eating nutritious food, and dealing with stress in healthy ways. People who take good care of themselves are less prone to suffering from psychiatric illnesses which is why self-care is necessary for everyone. It is especially important in those who are suffering from BPD because while it can not only worsen the symptoms, it can also result in slower recovery.

Many people tend to underestimate the importance of good sleep when it comes to proper self-care. If a person with BPD does not get adequate sleep they can become more anxious, irate, and aggressive. Here are some tips to help you get better sleep:

1. Avoid alcohol, nicotine, and caffeine a few hours before your bedtime. However, you will be able to sleep better if you completely eradicate these factors from your lifestyle.

2. Do not eat large meals before bedtime because it could cause upset stomach. Try to eat a light, filling meal at least three hours before you intend to go to sleep. On the other hand, don't go to bed with an empty stomach because a growling stomach caused by hunger can wake you up in the middle of the night and interfere with your sleep patterns. A warm glass of milk or a light snack are healthier alternatives.

3. Create a pre-bedtime ritual that will help you relax and soothe your mind. Some of these may include reading, aromatherapy, or taking a warm bath.

4. Establish a regular sleeping schedule which means avoiding naps, waking up at the same time each day, and sleeping at the same time every night.

5. Ensure that your bedroom is conducive to proper sleep. Lights should be turned off and noises reduced as much as possible. The temperature should also be just right.

People with borderline personality disorder should also pay close attention to diet and nutrition. Symptoms and moods can easily be affected by overeating, skipping meals, and eating food that have no nutritional value. Take supplements if needed, avoid fatty food, and make sure that you get a lot of fruits and vegetables in each day.

Exercise also has an impact on mental health, this is why more doctors recommend their patients to live an active lifestyle. In addition, regular workouts increase the release of endorphins in the body, which help you feel more elated. Exercise works for the person with BPD by providing a healthy outlet for stress and stabilizing one's mood. Setting fitness goals for yourself and achieving them will also boost self-esteem and confidence.

People who already suffer from BPD are less likely to take good care of their health and suffer from other disorders that arise from a sedentary and unhealthy lifestyle later on. These include arthritis, obesity, high blood pressure, chronic fatigue syndrome, back pain, and urinary incontinence. Those who suffer from BPD are known to have unhealthy lifestyles: smoking cigarettes, consumption of alcohol, lack of exercise and proper sleep, and a dependency on pain medication. The symptoms of borderline personality disorder causes people to make poorer lifestyle choices because of stressful events or genetics, which will cause serious health problems down the line. Furthermore, the link between one's physical health and borderline personality disorder can be complex although more research is being conducted on it.

Given these facts, there are still many things you can do to improve the state of your health. Pay close attention to unhealthy habits that you can change today, such as quitting smoking and reducing your alcohol intake. Studies have shown that people who were once diagnosed with BPD and who recovered successfully no longer report health issues. Getting treatment for BPD can significantly reduce your chances of developing physical ailments and creating good habits.

Medications are another important aspect of self-care for people with BPD. While many people think that medication does not constitute self-care, those who are not committed to taking their medications regularly or take the incorrect doses may only exacerbate their symptoms and slow down recovery time. Avoid making changes to your medication without consulting your physician. On a similar note, not taking your medication at all is unhealthy and can have dangerous side effects.

Managing stress properly is also part of self-care. The presence of stress may be inevitable in our daily lives, and it does not mean that it is automatically a negative element. The key here is to learn how to manage stress effectively. Sometimes, stress may feel overwhelming and during these times you may need additional help to overcome them.

Medication

Some doctors agree that medication is useful in the treatment of people with borderline personality disorder but others disagree. Today, there is still no medication that is licensed for the treatment of BPD. However, some forms of medicine have proven useful in reducing symptoms in certain people.

Usually, selective serotonin reuptake inhibitors (SSRI) are by default the first kind of medication that is prescribed to patients. SSRI's are designed to reduce impulsivity, depression, anger, suicidal behavior, and anxiety in people who suffer from mental health problems.

Medications such as anti-depressants and anti-anxiety pills may be useful to reduce symptoms especially during a crisis or emergency. The most common kinds of antidepressants prescribed for patients of borderline personality disorder include Prozac, Zoloft, Nardil, Wellbutrin, and Effexor. However, this kind of medication is not encouraged for long-term use particularly because depression and anxiety are often short-term symptoms that may come and go as a result of various stressors in a person's life.

Antipsychotics also have a positive effect on patients even though they don't suffer from BPD. These are effective in reducing paranoia, anxiety, hostility, anger, as well as impulsivity in people with borderline personality disorder. Common antipsychotic medications include Haldol, Clozaril, Risperdal, Seroquel, and Zyprexa.

Mood stabilizers are another form of medication that is used to treat symptoms of borderline personality disorder. These are effective in treating impulsivity, mood swings, and the intense changes in emotions caused by BPD.

Common types of mood stabilizers include Lithobid, Depakote, Tegretol, and Lamictal.

Medication that specializes in reducing anxiety are known as anxiolytics, and are also prescribed for BPD. While anxiolytics are given to patients of borderline personality disorder, there is still insufficient evidence on the effectiveness of these medications in treating BPD as a whole. In fact, there have been cases where certain types of anxiolytics, known as benzodiazepines, were shown to increase the symptoms of BPD in other people. Common types of anxiolytics used for BPD patients include Valium, Xanax, Ativan, Klonopin, and Buspar.

Studies are currently being done to test the effectiveness of other types of medication for borderline personality disorder. Findings from some studies have shown that taking supplements such as omega 3 fatty acids can reduce feelings of hostility and aggression in those suffering from BPD.

People with borderline personality disorder also need to be consistent in taking the medication as prescribed by their doctor. Honesty is also crucial in the success of medication for treating BPD. If you are taking care of someone, you may encourage this by reminding them to be open about their medication, what they feel, if they missed taking it, and other concerns they might have about it.

Before accepting medications from a physician, it is necessary to discuss any side effects thoroughly. If the side effects seem harmful, other forms of medicine may be considered especially if it is clear that the side effects are greater than the benefits. Medication used for borderline personality disorder may vary depending on the kind of medicine. Some of the common side effects are detailed below:

Antidepressants:

- Headache
- Insomnia
- Reduced appetite
- Sedation
- Sexual dysfunction
- Weight gain

Mood stabilizers:

- Acne
- Tremors
- Weight gain
- Gastrointestinal distress

Antipsychotics:

- Akathisia
- Dry mouth
- Weight gain
- Sexual dysfunction

- Sedation

Anti-anxiety:

- Fatigue
- Sleepiness
- Mental slowness
- Memory problems
- Impaired coordination

How To Know If A Medication Is Working

When you start to take medication for borderline personality disorder, this will result in both emotional and physical changes. If a medication is working well, the first thing that you may notice is a positive change in the way you respond to situations. Although the change is usually gradual and subtle, people experience the benefits of medications in a different time frame from other people. In fact, the positive changes are usually not felt unless they have been happening for some time. It is also common for other people to notice the changes in your emotional response before you do, so you may want to ask people that you are usually with if they notice any changes.

These are other indications to help you recognize when a medication is effective for you:

1. You no longer think about certain events or issues with the same frequency as before. Your pattern of thoughts is no longer inconsistent and no longer wanders from one subject to another. Although you may experience some fatigue when you begin treatment, there is a noticeable improvement on clarity and focus. It will also be easier to focus on one thought for a longer period of time.

2. Things, places, events, or people that used to be triggers no longer have the same effect on you. There will also be sudden improvements in communicating better with other people.

3. When you face situations that used to give you anxiety, you now face it with a sense of calmness. However, if you are taking benzodiazepines it is recommended to talk to your physician about this change in response.

4. Things that used to upset or anger you no longer elicits the same response.

Gender-Specific Treatment

Borderline personality disorder treatments focused on women are available to help them cope better because the way men and women manage their emotions when dealing with the illness will differ. This is why some patients prefer gender-specific treatment options. However, not all centers will have women-only treatment options available.

Each person's BPD case is as unique as their thumbprint. The important aspect of treatment is to find qualified professionals who can design a program that will be most effective for your individual needs and who may adapt as you start to recover from the illness.

Women who have borderline personality disorder are also at higher risk for developing co-occurring disorders such as eating disorders, anxiety, suicide, and depression. If you are experiencing these, it is necessary to find treatment that will also address co-occurring disorders.

Chapter 8: Common Misconceptions About Borderline Personality Disorder

If you or a loved one is diagnosed with borderline personality disorder, this may seem devastating or confusing at first. There are a lot of misconceptions surrounding BPD and what it really entails. There is also a stigma attached to being diagnosed with BPD, which is also the case with other psychological disorders. However, with 2 percent of the population being affected by BPD, it is actually more common than we realize. In fact, there are more people who are diagnosed with borderline personality disorder than there are with schizophrenia and bipolar disorder.

Here is a list of the common misconceptions about BPD:

- **Borderline personality disorder is not treatable**. It is difficult to deny the effectiveness of many treatment options for BPD. These are also backed up by numerous studies and research so there is no need to worry, indeed borderline personality disorder is a treatable condition.

- **Being diagnosed with borderline personality disorder is a life sentence.** There have been clinical studies documenting the progress of patients who underwent treatment for BPD. Many of them showed a significant improvement, in fact for some patients as much as 70% of the symptoms were reduced within 6 years after going through hospitalization and treatment. The reduction of symptoms meant that they no longer fulfilled the criteria required for one to be considered a patient of borderline personality disorder.

- **People who have BPD are manipulative.** Borderline personality disorder is a combination of a traumatic history with biological factors, resulting in a person's inability to regulate their own emotions. Although it is a fact that people who are emotional, such as those who are diagnosed with BPD, are more sensitive to situations in their environment, this doesn't mean that they are unable to manage their emotions completely. People with BPD may be seen as manipulative by those who are not properly educated about the illness since people in their immediate environment often have to make changes to adapt to them. But it should be remembered that individuals with BPD never actually make it a conscious decision to manipulate people. They simply resort to other behaviors when their own personal needs aren't met. When family members or other loved ones get burnt out from dealing with a person with BPD, the patient may resort to more extreme behaviors to get what they need unless they go through proper treatment.

- **Those who have BPD don't try hard enough to improve.** While borderline personality disorder is indeed treatable, just because it takes someone time to show improvement does not mean that they are not trying hard enough. There is a lot of cognitive, emotional, and behavioral dysregulation present which causes BPD in the first place. Treatment is aimed at addressing all of these symptoms and it is normal for improvement to take some time to manifest.

- **Only women have borderline personality disorder.** Although a majority of those diagnosed with BPD are women, many men are also affected by this disorder. Men are also usually underdiagnosed for BPD and other illnesses because women are more likely to seek the advice of a medical professional.

- **People with BPD are difficult to tolerate.** Many people find that those who have BPD are difficult to be around because they may be manipulative, controlling, too emotional, and destructive. It can be challenging to maintain healthy relationships with them but it is important for others to keep in mind that those with BPD have a hard time communicating their needs. People must keep in mind that individuals who live with BPD are genuinely going through suffering and do not act out of intention. They are often mistaken for simply having bad motives while lacking the will to improve. However, when people with BPD have access to proper treatment their symptoms can be reduced significantly. Family and friends can also participate in treatment options to help their loved one overcome BPD.

- **Borderline personality is a rare psychological illness.** The truth is that BPD is very common, affecting 2% of the American population. BPD is also more commonly occurring than Bipolar Disorder and schizophrenia combined.

Chapter 9: How To Choose The Right Therapist and Treatment for BPD

Effective treatment for borderline personality disorder is a combination of medication and therapy. This means that finding the right therapist to work with is crucial in the success of your treatment.

Treatment with BPD will entail meeting with your therapist 1 to 3 times a week depending on the severity of the condition. Therapy is usually long-term and your therapist understands that there are no quick fixes for addressing borderline personality disorder. A good BPD therapist is one who is committed to working with you, your family and your loved ones on a long-term basis. Additionally, a good BPD therapist is someone who has the skill and expertise in Dialectical Behavior Therapy. Other treatment options you may want to consider using in conjunction with DBT include supportive counseling, forms of psychotherapy, and cognitive behavioral therapy.

When you are in the process of finding a therapist to work with, it is important that you feel comfortable around them. Otherwise it would defeat the purpose because you wouldn't open up to someone whom you feel judges you or doesn't listen. In addition it is also necessary to ask questions about their work experience such as:

- How long have they been treating DBT?
- What kind of training have they had?
- Are they comfortable with taking phone calls outside session times?
- Do they accept insurance?
- How many other patients of BPD are they treating?

Before you decide on which therapist to work with, it is recommended to do a brief search of them on the internet. Most therapists have their own websites that provide information on the kind of treatment they specialize in, as well as their professional philosophy and interests. If you can obtain recommendations for good therapists to work with based on other people's experiences, this helps to validate a therapist' skills and effectiveness in treating BPD.

Once you have decided to inquire about a therapist, visit them at their office. Observe the way they handle phone calls and inquiries because that can say a lot about a person. In fact, a good and professional therapist will even encourage you to shop around until you find one that you are completely comfortable in working with.

If you are seeking help for a loved one whom you suspect has borderline personality disorder but hasn't been diagnosed yet, be wary about using this term. The therapist may have images of someone who is engaged in self-harm or suicide and may already have an approach in mind. Your loved one can receive better treatment if the therapist approaches the first few encounters with an open mind. Even if you suspect that it is BPD, the best thing to do is to describe the traits you are observing and leaving the diagnosis to the professionals.

Choosing a therapist who is skilled with the appropriate treatment methods for borderline personality disorder is important. However, studies have shown that this counts for only 15% of the success in treating BPD. The other 85% depends on the relationship between a therapist and a client. This is especially because patients of BPD already have fear of abandonment, and trust issues.

Another important consideration in the selection of a therapist is their availability and location. Convenience and driving time should be considered especially if you or your loved one may have a severe case of BPD and emergencies may arise. Therapy will only be effective if the clients can commit to being at appointments regularly, so if location will be an obstacle you are better off choosing a therapist that is in close proximity to your home.

Financing and payment are also important, so first determine how much you are willing to pay. If you already have health insurance it is recommended to call the insurance company to find out if they cover mental health benefits, outpatient treatment, and the number of sessions covered. In the event that your insurance provider would only cover certain therapists then they may be able to provide you with the list of those approved. Keep in mind that some therapists will only accept payments out of the patient's pocket. If the therapist you choose only has this payment option available, ask if they can provide you with an official receipt that you can send to your insurance provider for reimbursement. If the cost of therapy is above your budget, you can also try negotiating for lower fees.

The ideal situation is one where your loved one as the client, and the therapist, are able to form a therapeutic alliance. This is defined as a therapist-client relationship where the therapists are able to be empathic, provide unconditional and genuine care, and helps the patient trust him/her. With this kind of a relationship the client feels safe, understood, and respected by the therapist which greatly increases the chances for a successful treatment.

Inpatient or Outpatient Treatment Center

Inpatient and outpatient treatment options vary greatly and will have different impacts. It is important to determine which treatment option will be most effective for your loved one.

Inpatient treatment, in the form of a residential Borderline Personality Disorder treatment program, is recommended for individuals whose loved ones find that everyday life with borderlines are becoming too difficult to manage. It should also be considered as an option if you feel that you don't have the time due to family or work demands to provide your loved one with the care and support that they need to get better. An inpatient residential treatment program will provide your loved one with a nurturing environment where they will be asked to participate in various group and individual therapies.

In cases of extreme borderline personality disorder, admission to a psychiatric hospital may be necessary. This is especially important in the case of a mental health crisis such as when the individual is more prone to suicide and often has thoughts of harming other people. The care provided at a psychiatric hospital is more thorough as compared to inpatient or outpatient treatment facilities since they are designed to address extreme cases of BPD.

There are two kinds of psychiatric hospitals: inpatient and partial. At an inpatient psychiatric hospital, patients are required to stay during day and night where they will be given treatment. Patient's movements are some what limited, in fact they may not be allowed to leave their units when they first arrive. Inpatient psychiatric hospitals provide stability for people who are going through a severe mental health crisis and prevent them from committing suicide. The goal of an inpatient psychiatric hospital is to provide the patient with a stable, calm environment although hospitalization tends to last for a few months and for some, even years. But because research shows that longer hospitalizations do not necessarily mean more reductions in BPD symptoms, hospital stays for people with borderline personality disorder are now significantly shorter.

In a partial psychiatric hospital, individuals may come in treatment during the day but are not required to stay the night. This is because they are not prone to self-harm and dangerous behavior, so there is no need for medical staff to keep watch on them. Partial psychiatric hospitals help patients gradually achieve transition to their regular routine.

On the other hand, an outpatient treatment program will provide the same benefits as an inpatient program but offers more flexible schedules. It will allow your loved one to continue living and working as they need to, while receiving treatment with a set schedule of visits. It is also common for those who finish inpatient treatment programs to continue availing of outpatient treatment options as a form of support later on.

What to Expect in a Residential Treatment Facility

If you have made the decision to enter a residential treatment facility for borderline personality disorder, this is a big step towards recovery. Residential treatment facilities are excellent options in providing a healthy environment for people with BPD.

Residential treatment provides patients with full immersion towards BPD recovery. Clients are placed in their own private rooms where they are completely removed from triggers and stressors that they are normally faced with. It provides them with a chance to step back from their daily lives and focus completely on treating BPD. While not everyone who wishes to be treated for BPD can afford staying in a residential treatment facility for a long period of time, it is ideal for those who are having difficulties in managing their symptoms.

Once clients enter a residential treatment facility, they are assessed to determine exactly what their treatment needs are. Each person's case of borderline personality disorder may vary, as some people have more unique needs than others. The initial assessment is also used to check for the presence of other illnesses such as eating disorders, depression, and anxiety. Patients may be prescribed medication upon admission to immediately reduce symptoms of BPD, making them more receptive to therapy without added stress.

All therapeutic settings for patients of BPD share the same goal and that is to teach patients how to handle negative emotions, improve relationships, and enjoy better control in life. To meet these goals, clients are taught coping skills which are crucial to full recovery from borderline personality. Just like with any other new skill, these skills take time and dedication to fully comprehend. When patients put in more effort into the therapeutic process at the residential treatment facility, the faster they will be able to recover.

Residential treatment facilities will require patients to participate in regular sessions with a therapist. The combination of group and individual therapy is crucial to helping a borderline develop coping skills. Group therapy sessions also include a number of activities that can range from yoga, massage, acupuncture, and meditation.

For those who have the opportunity to stay at a residential treatment facility, there will also be chances to spend time alone and reflect on the healing process. This may be helpful for people especially those who need quiet time to think about the new life that awaits them, and how they can maximize the new life skills they are learning during treatment.

Once patients have completed their treatment, they should be committed to implementing changes in their daily lives. They also have the option of attending day treatment facilities to help them continue healing while on the road to recovery.

How to Prepare For An Appointment

If you or someone close to you is considering an appointment with a medical professional to seek help for borderline personality disorder, preparing for it ahead of time will help with diagnosis as well as treatment. Here are some things that can be done ahead of time to prepare for an appointment;

1. Create a list of the symptoms being experienced with an indication of how long they have been observed. When talking to a doctor, it is important to be as honest at all times when asked questions. Hiding things that you may not think are important because they are

embarrassing can prevent you from obtaining the best course of treatment.

2. Write all your relevant personal information that may help doctors identify if you are prone to developing BPD. These include any traumatic incidents that occurred in your past or recently, major stressors in life, and family medical history.

3. It is always recommended to bring along a loved one or close friend to an appointment. The moral support can help quell anxiety, fears, or nervousness which may be an obstacle to answering doctors' questions properly.

4. If prior to the appointment, you or loved ones already have questions about borderline personality disorder it's best to jot them down. This way you can ensure that you are making the most out of your appointment.

Chapter 10: Prognosis

If you are diagnosed with borderline personality disorder, this does not mean that you will have it for the rest of your life. Historically, mental health experts thought that being diagnosed with BPD was a life sentence. Thankfully, due to research and medical breakthroughs it is now possible to completely overcome borderline personality disorder and live a healthy, normal life again.

Most of the treatments used for BPD are proven effective in significantly reducing its symptoms.

Prognosis For Teenagers with BPD

More research is validating that the prognosis for adolescents with BPD are excellent. This is good news for parents as there are more chances that your teenager can recover completely from BPD.

Teenagers who were diagnosed as borderlines have high remission rates, with up to 85% of adolescents no longer meeting the diagnostic criteria for BPD 2 years after treatment. In fact, teens with BPD are more likely to recover and at a faster rate when compared to adults. Statistics show that 35% of adults will not meet the diagnostic criteria for borderline personality disorder after 2 years.

It is suspected that the reason why remission is so common in teenagers is because while they may show symptoms of borderline personality disorder, they don't actually have the illness. It is common for teens to exhibit the same behaviors described in those with BPD, such as mood swings, aggression, and extremely impulsive behavior. This is especially true if they are going through puberty and / or dealing with a stressful situation. However, when these environmental and biological factors are reduced, so do the symptoms.

However there are some factors that lead to a poor prognosis for BPD in teenagers. If a teenager exhibits symptoms of antisocial personality behavior before they reach 15 years of age, they are at higher risk for developing BPD later on.

Chapter 11: How Family and Friends Can Help

Borderline personality disorder may seem like a mystery even to family and friends who want to help a loved one. It is easy to feel overwhelmed and at a loss on how you can help someone manage BPD better. But don't worry: there are proven strategies that you can use to support your loved one and even improve your overall relationship with them.

The personalities of those with BPD may exhibit mild or severe symptoms. It's usually those closest to them who can identify the extent of the illness. Living with someone who has BPD may even be described as an emotional rollercoaster, because you will have to deal with it too. Read on below to learn how to obtain treatment for them.

Create a Plan: The situation may be overwhelming in the beginning, but it's important for you to start slow. Take a deep breath, understand that everything will be alright, and that you are merely starting the process of recovery. It will not happen overnight but your patience and dedication is crucial to the success of the treatment. Start creating your plan by compiling a list of nearby Borderline Personality Treatment centers in your area. Call them and visit each one to find the treatment center that's best for your loved one's needs.

While you don't have to visit them all in one day, it is best to plan your schedule so that you still have time to attend to your responsibilities.

Ask Questions: When visiting a BPD treatment center, feel free to ask all the questions you need. Whether it's a concern about the facilities, fees, or needing additional information on borderline personality disorder itself, go ahead and ask it. If early on you feel overwhelmed by all the questions you had in mind, have a list ready so that you avoid forgetting important questions.

Asking the right questions at BPD treatment centers will give you a sense of the professionalism and knowledge of the staff. It will help you make a better-informed decision on the situation as a whole and choosing the proper facilities needed, since not all BPD patients have the same needs.

Here are some topics you inquire about when visiting a BPD treatment facility:

- Dialectical Behavior Therapy options
- Holistic treatment options (meditation and yoga)
- Treatment of co-occurring disorders
- Support programs for families
- Individual and group therapies
- Continued support for patients after BPD treatment

Relationships With People Who Have BPD

The mere concept of relationships can cause anxiety to people who have borderline personality disorder. Relationships are successful when two people come together regardless of their opinions, quirks, and personalities. They begin when something unexplained clicks, bringing together two people who come from different walks of life.

The honeymoon stage occurs early on in the relationship, and for many these are usually considered the best days. During the honeymoon period, couples are still so in love and exert the extra effort to make the other person feel that they are loved too. Eventually, the honeymoon period will die down and people get more comfortable with one another. As the layers are stripped off, people begin to reveal their true selves to their partners. Once barriers are broken down, this paves the way for misunderstandings and oftentimes one partner may end up feeling neglected.

While relationships can be difficult for everyone, it is no surprise that people with borderline personality disorder have a pattern of broken or strained relationships. The symptoms of BPD that make relationships difficult to manage include fear of abandonment, reckless behavior, paranoia, and difficulties regulating thoughts and emotions. In order to make a relationship work, these symptoms of borderline personality disorder place added pressure on the usual challenges that people in relationships already face. In fact, individuals with BPD may resort to self-harm and suicide, substance abuse, and eating disorders which will make relationships more difficult.

If you find out that you are already in a relationship with someone who has borderline personality disorder, it is important to remember that it's not the end. If you truly love someone, you will not give up on them despite them having BPD. There is hope despite the challenges that borderline personality disorder brings in relationships but you and your partner can learn how to communicate better.

It is Dialectical Behavior Therapy that is most useful for those who are in relationships. It combines tenets of Cognitive Behavioral Therapy with elements of Buddhism to help those who are suffering from BPD. Dialectical Behavior Therapy, also referred to as DBT, teaches skills that are crucial in any relationship. These include distress tolerance, mindfulness, emotional regulation, and effectiveness in interpersonal relationships.

How To Know If Someone You Are Dating Has BPD

Dating doesn't have to be complicated, but it is clear that when a person becomes too clingy this can damage the relationship. If you are dating someone who has borderline personality disorder, you may experience clinginess in extreme cases.

However, because people with BPD are afraid of being alone, they will resort to desperate measures to stay in the relationship no matter what happens. Dating someone with BPD may mean that your partner will go to lengths in order to obtain your approval. It is very rare that they will disagree with you, since they are easily influenced by your thoughts and opinions. Individuals who have BPD have a fear of abandonment by their partner and are constantly in a state of anxiety, fear, and sadness. If you are dating someone with BPD it is necessary to understand their needs and ensure that your needs are balanced too.

Determining if the person you are dating has BPD is the first step before you change your approach to them. Warning signs to look out for include:

- Difficulty starting projects
- Needs validation from other people before making decisions

- Needs the help of other people in taking responsibility for different areas of their life
- Going to extreme lengths in order to get other people's approval and support
- Feels helpless when it comes to taking care of themselves

If people with BPD are not treated, this can prevent them from reaching their true potential because they are dependent on someone else to support them. Common characteristics of people with BPD are those that have never experienced living alone and independently, and have never had a job that paid them enough money to sustain themselves. They are also passive in their dependency and surround themselves with enablers, a behavior that prevents them from having successful long-term relationships.

If a person with BPD goes through a breakup, they feel helpless and need other people to take care of them. They have low self-esteem which makes them more prone to other mental health illnesses, even resorting to drug and substance abuse as a means of coping.

Once you see these signs in the person you are dating, understand that the situation is not impossible to mend. Encourage your partner to get help in the form of treatment for borderline personality disorder.

Friendships With People Who Have BPD

If you have a good friend who has borderline personality disorder, you may have witnessed uncomfortable behavior and want to learn how to cope with it. Individuals with BPD have difficulties regulating their emotions, a characteristic that often puts a strain on relationships with those close to them. You may feel like you have been judged, lied to, or manipulated by a friend with BPD.

In order to avoid being on the receiving end of your friend's destructive behavior, you can learn how to set boundaries. It is up to you to decide what kind of behavior you will and will not tolerate from them. Having the initiative to set boundaries to protect yourself and save your friendship does not mean you are a bad friend. Before you save someone else, it is important that you also take care of yourself while you prevent getting caught up in negative emotions and drama.

Remember that you and your friend were pulled together for a reason. This may be because you had shared things in common, or because your personalities complemented each other. Friendships are formed because in another person we see a mirror or someone whose strengths make up for our weaknesses. Even if a person is borderline they can still be intelligent, funny, and spontaneous individuals who are a lot of fun to be around. However, when their BPD symptoms begin to exacerbate it may be time for you to step forward.

You may end up being dumped on with negative emotions when your friend is feeling extremely stressed and needs to let it out. In the beginning you probably did your best to be there for a friend whenever they needed to rant about a bad relationship, stress at work, or other things that cause them to feel pain. But if they cannot seem to do anything to address the situation and ends up venting to you time and again, you may feel emotionally exhausted with nothing to give back anymore.

Remember that for a person who lives with BPD, their lives are in a constant state of conflict. They may feel the need to vent about it to people close to them which makes you an outlet for their stress, causing burden to you. This is why it has become necessary for friends of those with BPD to learn how to establish boundaries.

Setting boundaries can be challenging because people with BPD are known to be hyper sensitive. There are ways you can set boundaries with love and affection. The ideal goal here is that your friend will learn to manage their expectations over time so that you are no longer the dump site for their problems and stress.

In the process of setting boundaries, choose your words carefully. You can begin by saying something like "I value our friendship and truly care for you, but it is causing me stress when I constantly hear about your conflicts. I will always support you, but please try to work on the issues and keep me posted on a weekly basis." Be prepared for an emotional outburst but stay patient with the process. Keep in mind that you are not responsible for your friend's actions but you can work on saving the friendship by assuring them of your love and care.

Chapter 12: BPD and Suicide

While the topic of suicide tends to make people uncomfortable, it is a fact that we have to face head on especially if you have a loved one who has been diagnosed with borderline personality disorder. A staggering 80% of people with BPD have attempted suicide at least once in their lifetime and this is something that should not be taken lightly. The suicide success rate of those with BPD is much higher than those of other psychiatric disorders but if you keep yourself informed you can stop it in its tracks.

The first step in helping prevent suicide is by identifying the warning signs associated that your loved one may be contemplating suicide:

- Difficulty concentrating
- Sudden change in attitude
- Lack of interest in enjoyable activities
- Talking about suicide
- Substance and alcohol abuse
- Change in sleeping and eating patterns

It is also common for suicidal people to act as though they are happy, but this is followed by periods of deep depression. If you think that someone you love is suicidal due to borderline personality disorder, there are things you can do to help. These include:

- Advising them not to kill themselves since it is important to a suicidal person to hear that you don't want them to die
- Ask questions about the feelings they have and encourage them to talk about it
- Help them validate their positive experiences
- Ask how you can help them
- Remove all weapons and items in your home that may assist in suicide
- Communicate to them the confidence you have that they will overcome their crisis
- In the event of an emergency, call 911

Most importantly, approach the situation with as much empathy and compassion to help a suicidal friend, family member, partner, or relative. Although this is an unfortunate effect of borderline personality disorder, it is possible to help a person overcome it and encourage them to live a normal life again. It is also necessary to observe someone you love if you suspect that they are suicidal so you can identify clues as to when they are feeling down and more prone to committing suicide.

Self-Mutilation

Self-mutilation is the act of intentionally causing injury on one's body. It is also referred to as self-harm, self-injury, cutting, and violence. Self-mutilation is a symptom of psychiatric illness and is manifested by those who suffer from extreme cases of borderline personality disorder. It is different from suicide because while self-harm is present there is no intent to kill oneself. However, self-mutilation is serious because it may lead to fatal consequences and even death.

Oftentimes it is difficult to determine when someone you love is mutilating themselves. Similar to cases of eating disorders wherein people go to great lengths to keep their symptoms a secret from everyone else, self-mutilation may be hard to spot. This is why it may be necessary to keep a close watch on someone you love especially if you think that they are prone to self-harm. Symptoms to watch out for include:

- Scars from cuts or burns
- Broken bones
- Fresh cuts
- Bruises
- Bald spots
- Keeping sharp objects
- Spending too much time alone
- Using long-sleeved clothing even in warm weather to mask cuts on arms
- Using excuses of accidents to explain cuts and scratches

Self-mutilation is different from other widely practiced forms of artistic expression which include body piercings and the use of tattoos. Self-mutilation is an unhealthy method of coping when a person with borderline personality disorder is experiencing extreme, overwhelming emotions including anger, fear, shame, sadness, and rage.

People who resort to self-mutilation are often highly impulsive in nature. They tend to be provoked by triggers, resulting in an urge to hurt themselves. In many people suffering from BPD, self-mutilation is a ritualistic behavior and is not done just once. People with BPD may resort to self-mutilation in a planned manner and usually carry it out in a very methodical way.

The most frequently harmed body parts with self-mutilation are the arms and legs. This is because these two areas can easily be covered up by clothing, and can also be reached in order to perform acts of self-injury. However, any other part of the body may also be affected with self-harm.

Cutting is the most common method of self-mutilation, where an individual uses a blade, knife, or scissors to cause a wound. Other forms of self-mutilation include:

- Overdosing
- Poisoning

- Hitting or punching oneself
- Banging one's head
- Pinching
- Biting
- Pulling out hair
- Biting nails
- Carving on skin
- Burning

Self-harming brings about a temporary sense of release for those with borderline personality disorder. Episodes are followed by intense feelings of shame and guilt, and the painful emotions they try to hide will return. Self-mutilation is an unhealthy coping mechanism that doesn't discriminate with gender and age; as long as they are suffering from a mental health disorder they are prone to self-mutilation if they are not receiving proper treatment.

Self-harm is more common in those who also suffer from drug and alcohol abuse because it allows them to carry it out easily without feeling the pain instantly.

Chapter 13: How To Help Yourself if You Have BPD

If you have borderline personality disorder, it is necessary to take that first step to seek medical care even though it may be difficult in the beginning. It is important to realize that you can get better with treatment despite the fact that being diagnosed with BPD may be overwhelming and frustrating in the beginning.

Living with borderline personality disorder does not have to be stressful. To make it manageable, it is necessary to commit to the treatment prescribed after your doctor has diagnosed you with borderline personality disorder. Therapy can provide you with valuable life lessons which will teach you how to cope with mood swings and control emotions that otherwise would be difficult to manage.

Everyone's experience with borderline personality disorder may vary and because of this medication may or may not be prescribed in conjunction with therapy. If your doctor prescribes medication it will be used to mitigate the most harmful effects of BPD such as anxiety and depression. Medications combined with therapy can help you more effectively deal with the ups and downs of life that arise from the symptoms of borderline personality disorder. As a result, you will be able to have clear thinking space and maximize the therapy provided for you.

Commitment to therapy can't be emphasized enough: this can make or break the healing process. It is the most important thing that you can do to manage living with borderline personality disorder. The illness can cause people to experience extreme emotions and even resort to self-destructive behavior as a means of coping and masking emotions. Committing to therapy will help you learn how to cope in a healthy manner. Otherwise, you may continue living in a world where you constantly succumb to emotional triggers and struggle with your own personal relationships. It will be a constant cycle of challenges and pain.

On top of treatment and medication, one major aspect that will truly help you in your journey towards healing is the moral support from your loved ones. Family, friends, relatives, coworkers, and significant others can all provide you with the strength that you need to manage borderline personality disorder. Just like getting over any serious mental or physical illness, the recovery period could be a lengthy and challenging process but the support of loved ones can make it much easier.

If you begin treatment for borderline personality disorder, honest conversations about the process with those close to you can help relieve anxiety and stress. Don't be afraid to ask them to support you in your process. Borderline personality disorder can place a strain on relationships with people in your life, but asking them to understand and get involved can help them identify what they can also do to help you. Communication is a two-way process, and initiating a dialogue on changes you can make with someone important in your life will lift a great load off your shoulders.

If your family prefers not to get involved in helping you with your treatment, this is not a sign for you to give up. You can still move forward with the many support groups found in your local mental health center or community. You may be able to form a valuable network of people who are going through the same experience and can provide you with the support that you need.

As long as you go through the diagnosis, treatment, medication, and support, there is no reason that you can't enjoy a normal life again. You are on your way to living in a world where you can enjoy healthy, stable relationships.

In addition, there are also other things you can do that will contribute to improving your situation:

- Discuss various treatment options with your doctor and ask all the questions you have in mind. Once you are given treatment, be as disciplined as possible and stick to the treatment schedules.
- Make an effort to stick to a healthy lifestyle with proper nutrition, exercise, and sleep.
- To help reduce the stress or anxieties of treatment, talk to friends or engage in constructive activities such as hobbies or exercise.
- Set goals for each day and break down large tasks into smaller, manageable ones. You will feel better about being able to accomplish something each day.
- Identify the situations, places, or people that make you feel better about yourself. Spend more time doing things that make you happy provided that these are not dangerous or will make the situation worse such as engaging in drugs or drinking alcohol.
- Keep yourself informed with all that you can find out regarding borderline personality disorder. Being in the dark about BPD may make you uneasy and trigger anxiety.

If you don't know where to begin asking for help, talk to a doctor. You can also talk to other people who can offer help, which include:

- Outpatient clinics
- Employee assistance programs at your office
- Local psychiatric societies
- Hospital psychiatric departments
- Community mental health centers
- Private clinics

Resisting the Urge to Cut

The urge to harm oneself is a symptom of borderline personality disorder that should be managed properly. This can be carried out in different ways such as burning, pulling hair out, and banging your head. If you are diagnosed with BPD you may already be familiar with self-harm but there are ways you can overcome it although it may feel like a major challenge in the beginning.

1. Make yourself aware of situations or circumstances that provoke you to cut. For people with BPD, cutting is an impulsive act and provides a temporary solution for overwhelming emotions. Talking to your therapist can help you identify these triggers and how to deal with them in a healthy manner.

2. Have a list of things that soothe and relax you. Each time you feel an urge to cut, do one of the activities that let you feel good. Cutting often results in feelings of guilt and shame afterward, but engaging in activities that make you feel good will result in a more permanent high. These activities may include taking a warm bath, reading a book, listening to music, or exercising.

3. Keep in mind that the urge to cut is merely a feeling that will pass. While the trigger provokes a sense of darkness, try to simply wait out the moment until it has passed completely.

4. Understand that recovery will take time, so be patient with yourself. Your goals should be realistic because behaviors will not change overnight. Your negative emotions do not define you, it is a matter of being committed to the positive change and a better life that awaits.

Self-Soothing

If you live with borderline personality disorder, you are most likely feeling distressed most of the time. You may have a skewed perception of the way other people react and behave. You are prone to living in fear of abandonment from those that are close to you, and constantly experience self-loathing.

Because of these extreme emotions it has become especially important for people with borderline personality disorder to resort to self-soothing.

Learning how to self-soothe will prevent you from attempting to control others as a method of coping.

Self-soothing refers to the ability to consciously calm yourself down when you are overwhelmed with your emotions. People are capable of self-soothing even when they aren't conscious about it, but for those who have BPD it may take time and effort to learn this skill. When you practice self-soothing you will know that the negative emotional state you are currently experiencing is only temporary.

You can resort to self-soothing by doing simple things such as taking a long walk, enjoying a warm bath, watching a movie or listening to music as a form of escapism, or talk to a friend that you trust. Even though these activities seem so simple, they are effective in helping you return to a more stable mindset. Additionally, these methods of self-soothing are perfectly natural and healthy ways of coping with the emotional intensity that BPD brings about.

Self-soothing provides an outlet for people with BPD to deal with emotions positively. Without it, people end up resorting to unhealthy activities such as substance abuse, alcoholism, isolation, depression, rage, and self-harm. In order to release pent-up negative emotions, they resort to destructive behavior that harms them and those that love them because they don't think about the consequences of their actions. As a result the emotional pain is intensified rather than resolved.

The practice of self-soothing techniques can aid in the successful recovery from borderline personality disorder. The goal of treatment is to teach people with BPD that the emotional intensity they are feeling are temporary and that it is possible to redirect their energies into something more productive.

People who suffer from BPD are vulnerable to feeling empty and lack a strong sense of self. When you engage in therapy and activities that make you feel good, such as with self-soothing techniques, these negative feelings can be addressed properly. Once you accept that you deserve all the love and care instead of succumbing to anxiety and depression, you can begin to take better care of yourself. When learning self-soothing techniques, it is important that you are patient with yourself. Over time, these activities can turn into healthy habits if you are dedicated. The end goal of self-soothing techniques is achieving control over intense emotional states and eventually recovering successfully from borderline personality disorder.

Chapter 14: Alternative Methods of Treatment

There are many things you can do to help yourself heal from borderline personality disorder through various alternative forms of treatment, which we will go over in detail below. Remember that these should not be perceived as a stand-alone alternative to medication and proper treatment. Rather, they should be used in conjunction with other forms of treatment which you can also utilize when you are in the recovery stage.

Mindfulness Meditation

Recently, more doctors, therapists, and mental health professionals have validated the benefits of mindfulness meditation in treating a number of illnesses including borderline personality disorder, chronic pain, depression, and anxiety.

Mindfulness meditation is defined as the ability to purposely pay attention to the present moment without judgment. Practicing mindfulness meditation allows you to be aware of the moment and of all things happening internally such as thoughts, feelings, and emotions; as well as externally such as things that you smell, see, and hear. However the most important aspect of mindfulness meditation is the approach of everything without judgment. This means paying close attention to all that is happening without labeling them as either good or bad.

The concept of mindfulness comes from Buddhism, although recently mindfulness practice has become widespread all over the world. Mindfulness is perceived today as a skill that can be used outside of its Eastern religious roots because of its numerous benefits.

Mindfulness meditation is particularly beneficial for people who are living with borderline personality disorder because they often experience intense emotions and may feel stuck with these negative feelings. People with BPD also see the world in black and white, the very form of judgment that mindfulness meditation practice aids in removing. When people with BPD practice mindfulness meditation they can learn how to cope with situations in a normal, healthy manner. It allows you to create a space where you can notice the emotion you are feeling and allow you to be aware how you are reacting to a specific situation or trigger.

For example, getting into an argument with a friend can provoke feelings of anger and rage. People who are not trained at mindfulness will end up acting on these feelings without thinking about the negative consequences that may arise. Mindfulness meditation practice helps one to be aware of the emotions you are feeling and step back from it.

Additionally, there are several scientific studies that support the benefits of mindfulness meditation in treating borderline personality disorder. Treatment should affect the amygdala, neurotransmitters, and the prefrontal cortex which are parts of the brain responsible for the behavior of people with borderline personality disorder. Mindfulness has been shown to be effective in addressing structural and functional changes in the brain that increase positive emotions, reduce pain, and promote better overall health making it an excellent method of alternative treatment for people with BPD.

There are forms of mindfulness meditation practice which focus on activating parts of the prefrontal cortex, which doesn't function well in people with borderline personality disorder. Different types of mindfulness practice have been shown to stimulate various parts of the prefrontal cortex. Similarly, certain types of exercise can improve the way a body looks in different ways. The bottom line is that all kinds of mindfulness practice are effective in strengthening the circuits within the prefrontal cortex while reducing the reactivity of the amygdala. If you opt for this method of alternative treatment for borderline personality disorder, you can choose from different types such as transcendental meditation, zazen, or basic mindfulness meditation.

Currently, mindfulness meditation is already a component of psychotherapies such as Dialectical Behavior Therapy, Mindfulness Based Cognitive Therapy, and Mindfulness Based Stress Reduction.

The benefits of mindfulness meditation when used to treat borderline personality disorder include:

- Improve the perception of oneself
- Change reactions to fear, pain, and anger
- Address thoughts that are caused by pain

When the practice of mindfulness activates the prefrontal cortex, it produces a painkilling opiate known as endorphins. The presence of endorphins in the brain reduces pain, decreases fear, and increase the overall feeling of joy and happiness.

Yoga Therapy

Various forms of yoga, when used together with medication and treatment, can help expedite a cure from BPD symptoms. The practice of yoga has helped many people manage the symptoms of borderline personality disorder more effectively. Because of this, many psychiatric centers also offer yoga classes to supplement therapy. However, it should be remembered that while yoga has significant benefits it is not advisable to practice it without the supervision of a teacher. Some poses may be strenuous and can result in injury if they are practiced without proper guidance. Any medical conditions should also be discussed with your yoga teacher beforehand.

Kundalini yoga's effects have been promising in the reduction of symptoms for borderline personality disorder. The practice of kundalini helps one release pent up energy, leaving one to feel soothed and calm after each class. While kundalini yoga may be mentally and physically intense for those who aren't used to yoga, it is valued for its spiritual benefits because sessions involve chanting hymns. Kundalini yoga also includes breathing exercises, and all sessions end with meditation.

Sudarshan kriya is another type of yoga that is popular for those suffering from borderline personality disorder. The practice of Sudarshan kriya is a combination of breathing exercises and yoga poses, which have been proven effective in reducing the symptoms of depression. Sudarshan kriya was developed by same creator of the Art of Living foundation, and to practice one must enroll in their courses.

Breathing Exercises

Therapists usually advise their clients to take deep breaths and relax. More than a way of telling them to calm down, therapists do this because there are significant benefits that breathing exercises can bring especially for those who are diagnosed with borderline personality disorder. The medical term for it is known as Resonance Frequency Paced Breathing, a process that teaches patients how to slow down regular breathing by taking a few deep breaths at a time. The healthy rate for most people is 10 to 12 breaths in a minute. Resonance Frequency Paced Breathing can help bring this down to 6 breaths per minute.

There are many studies that back up the effectiveness of breathing exercises such as this. One is that since the heart rate reflects how we perceive a threat, it will beat much faster as a response to stress resulting in a tight, pounding feeling in the chest. People with borderline personality disorder suffer from a lower heart rate variability which is defined as lower rates of calming down once the stressor or threat has passed. Lower heart rate can result in many other problems such as issues with flexibility, interfering with emotional regulation, higher levels of stress, and difficulty concentrating.

Because the core symptom of BPD is difficulty in regulating emotions, breathing exercises provides a safe alternative treatment in dealing with stressors. However, Resonance Frequency Paced Breathing is a new breathing technique and some people with BPD still find it challenging to slow down their breathing.

There are many other forms of breathing exercises that are also available with alternative methods of treatment such as yoga and meditation.

Exercise

Getting regular exercise has been a tried and tested way of reducing stress and anxiety no matter how old you are. There are many other benefits such as keeping your body fit, and helping you get a better night's rest. New research today shows that exercise is actually beneficial in supplementing therapy to cure mental illnesses including borderline personality disorder.

Individuals with BPD are encouraged to talk to their therapists about including exercise over the course of their treatment. In fact, during initial discussions with therapists, some patients may report having an athletic history or communicating that being active has always been an important part of their lives. Psychiatric professionals have confirmed the positive effects of integrating exercise in treatment in many forms of mental illnesses.

Those battling with depression, for instance, may find exercise the least enjoyable activity to engage in. However, starting out with just 30 minutes a week of physical activity can already help one feel better. Patients can then gradually increase the frequency and intensity of exercise especially when they find an activity that they are more comfortable with. Not everyone enjoys going to the gym, for instance, and finds that yoga, badminton, boxing, or pilates is much more enjoyable. There are no limitations to the kind of exercise you can do, as long as you enjoy it these will reap benefits both physically and mentally.

Regardless of the kind of workout that you choose, the important part is to stick to it regularly. Create a weekly routine where you make time for it, whether it be a few days a week or on the weekends. Soon enough you will see that exercise is effective in stabilizing your mood and improving your health. However, just like with other alternative methods of therapy exercise should not be seen as a cure-all but should work together with treatment and prescribed medication from your doctor.

Expressive Writing

Expressive writing has been shown to have a positive impact on people who suffer from psychological as well as physical problems. In fact the practice of expressive writing has been used for centuries as a way of dealing with stress because it provides catharsis and encourages personal discovery. It is one of the most effective methods of coping with borderline personality disorder.

Expressive writing involves writing about experiences as a way of understanding and communicating your personal responses and emotions. There are many forms of expressive writing such as the use of a blog, diary, or poetry. Regardless of the type of expressive writing you choose, you can still benefit from it. If it helps you to share the thoughts you jot down, you may do so; otherwise it's perfectly fine to keep the contents private.

The practice of expressive writing is useful for people with borderline personality disorder because it helps people make sense of events in their life. It provides an outlet where one can process events and what they mean. Writing down thoughts and feelings also help release any pent up emotions you may have, thereby helping you feel better about situations.

Sharing what you write may be a means of social support. Some people find that they express their feelings better when they write them down as opposed to discussing them. Perhaps this is attributed to the fact that expressive writing gives one more space and time to think about emotions and choosing words that describe one's experiences. Receiving positive feedback about what you have written will also allow you to feel better about yourself.

Although there are no hard rules when it comes to expressive writing, the idea is to write down events that are important to you and reflect on it. These events are usually those that triggered a deep emotional response and are relevant to you. You could begin by writing about a stressful day at work that prompted you to feel negative emotions. You may also choose to write about past experiences such as an event that occurred in your childhood which causes you to feel pain to this day. Keep in mind that the topic you choose to write about isn't as important when compared to how you write it. Expressive writing is effective when you write about an event in depth, exploring all the feelings, thoughts, and emotions associated with the topic.

Acupuncture

Acupuncture is an ancient method of healing which originated in China more than 3,500 years ago. Today it remains to be one of the most widely used natural healing techniques for a variety of illnesses. Acupuncture is used to treat both physical and mental disorders without any side effects. The foundation of acupuncture is based on the ancient Chinese belief that the "Qi" or energy flows through the body and is responsible for the state of one's mind or body. The Qi passes through the 20 meridians in the body, all of which affect the organs. Chinese medicine dictates that illness occurs when there is an imbalance in the flow of Qi, thereby the use of acupuncture to restore the correct flow will address the illness.

The body contains over 2,000 acupuncture points where the Qi can be stimulated through the use of a needle to restore one back to health. Treatment through acupuncture requires several sessions lasting anywhere from a few weeks or months. Those with borderline personality disorder may benefit from acupuncture treatment because it has the ability to stimulate the nervous system and cause the body to release more endorphins, also known as happy hormones. The presence of endorphins in the body will also alleviate pain, both physical and emotional.

Music Therapy

Music therapy has shown to have positive effects in treating mood and anxiety disorders. Music therapy can also be customized to treat isolation, depression, teach communication skills and encourage socialization. The goal of music therapy is to get the patient involved in singing, playing musical instruments, and other creative activities that are designed to change the way a person responds and behaves. A skilled music therapist creates the environment where the patient can enjoy a positive interaction and allow them to express themselves in a healthy manner.

Aromatherapy

Aromatherapy is used to treat a wide range of illnesses, prevent sickness, and promote calmness and relaxation. It is the use of various fragrant oils that have been extracted from plants that have known medicinal benefits. People with borderline personality disorder are encouraged to integrate aromatherapy in their life because of its mood stabilizing and soothing benefits.

By inhaling the aroma of these oils, they release a scent that enters the body by passing through the respiratory system and stimulating the nerves that are connected to the brain's limbic region. The limbic area is responsible for emotions, learning, and memory, which is why aromatherapy is particularly useful for those who are suffering from mental disorders and are seeking alternative methods of treatment. When aromatherapy is done correctly and practiced regularly, studies have shown that it can result in significant psychological changes.

Aromatherapy oils that are recommended for alleviating symptoms of BPD include:

- Lavender
- Juniper
- Chamomile
- Basil
- Angelica

- Spikenard
- Marjoram
- Clary Sage

If aromatherapy interests you, here are important things to keep in mind:

1. Research thoroughly before you purchase essential oils. High quality therapeutic grade essential oils usually come in blue or brown bottles, since clear bottles let light in which can affect the quality of the oil.

2. Aromatherapy oils must be used with caution as many of them may be poisonous when consumed or come into contact with mucous surfaces such as the eyes or open wounds. While essential oils are 100% natural, they are concentrated forms of plants and are meant to be taken correctly only through inhalation. Some essential oils are extremely strong and need to be diluted before use especially if they are to be applied directly on the skin.

3. Educate yourself on the various ways you can use aromatherapy. While inhalation is the most famous method of aromatherapy, baths, massages, and compresses are also useful.

Chapter 15: Nutrition

It is a known fact that poor nutrition can contribute to a number of illnesses. Apart from hypertension, obesity, and cancer; poor nutrition can also provoke and worsen the symptoms of many psychological illnesses including borderline personality disorder. Very few people understand the connection between depression and nutrition because there is a stronger emphasis on the connection between physical illness and diet.

Statistics show that 1 in 4 Americans are diagnosed with a mental health disorder, which translates to almost 60 million people. These mental health disorders have become the leading cause of disabilities in the country. Treatment usually consists of medication, which may have unwanted side effects as discussed earlier. In some instances, side effects may be extremely severe and life threatening which has prompted the general population to seek out alternative methods of treatment for psychiatric illnesses including borderline personality disorder.

Medical professionals have also noticed that the increase of mental health illnesses in the Western world occurred simultaneously to the deterioration of nutrition. In other words, more Americans are making poor choices leading to a significantly higher incidence in mental health problems. Additionally, the Western diet has become notorious for a reduced intake of fruits and vegetables which adds to more nutritional deficiencies.

The most common nutritional deficiencies evident in patients of mental health disorders include Omega 3 fatty acids, minerals, B vitamins, and other amino acids which are crucial to neurotransmitter activity in the brain. Population studies provide conclusive evidence on the correlation of a high fish intake to a low incidence in mental disorders as a result of fish consumption in certain societies. Healthy individuals are recommended to take up to 2 grams of Omega 3 fatty acids daily although those with mental health disorders should take up to 9.5 mg to make up for the deficiencies.

When treating mental disorders, a proper diagnosis and thorough discussion of the treatment options should be made available to the patient. At the end of the day, the patient should have the right to choose if they would like to take additional supplements. There is clearly more interest in nutritional treatment as well as holistic therapy. In this section we will go over various nutritional supplements and herbs that are recommended for patients of borderline personality disorder.

Omega-3 Fatty Acids

Numerous studies have validated the mood stabilizing benefits of Omega 3 fatty acids. It is particularly important for brain health, since this part of the body contains the highest amount of lipids or fat. The brain's lipids are made up of fatty acids and are primary constituents of its membranes. The gray matter in our brain is made up of 50% polyunsaturated fatty acids, a majority of which fall under the Omega 3 category which are supplemented by one's diet.

Omega 3 fatty acids are present in a wide range of food, particularly seafood. These compounds are also commonly referred to as fish oil, supplements of which are available in supplement form.

Mental health illnesses are not caused by a single thing rather they are a combination of biological and environmental factors. In some situations a person has higher biological risk of developing borderline personality disorder and when coupled with environmental factors such as a strenuous life event this may provoke the incidence of BPD. For example, systemic inflammation, a biological process that occurs depending on a person's stress levels is known to increase a person's risk for developing borderline personality disorder. The consumption of Omega 3 fatty acids can significantly reduce the effects of systemic inflammation, leading scientists to view Omega 3 fatty acids as an effective supplement in treating people with BPD and many other mental illnesses.

Omega 3 fatty acids are already recommended for those suffering from depression, one of the most common co-occurring illnesses with borderline personality disorder. Research shows that people with extreme depression also have incidences of systemic inflammation which can be directly addressed through the consumption of Omega 3 fatty acids. Additionally, other studies conclude that those with suicidal tendencies also have lower amounts of Omega 3 fatty acids in their brain. Many people who resort to taking Omega 3 fatty acid supplements report feeling better, with a significant decrease in their symptoms. In fact, even women who suffer from postpartum depression are prescribed to take Omega 3 supplements.

For most people receiving treatment for borderline personality disorder, Omega 3 fatty acids are highly recommended as additional supplements together with their medication and forms of treatment. It is not meant to be taken as a stand-alone medication especially in extreme cases. However, consuming it can speed up the healing process and reduce the vulnerability of a person in suffering from side effects caused by a dependency on other drugs.

Herbs

Yerba Mate

Yerba Mate is an herb that comes from Argentina which is known for its mood-stabilizing properties. It is also known for its anti-depressant and anti-anxiety properties, making it an ideal supplement for treating borderline personality disorder. In fact it is common practice in Argentina to feed yerba mate to children who are temperamental because it is effective in soothing them. Other benefits of yerba mate include reduction of fatigue and increasing energy.

Many people who take yerba mate report feeling happy because it can significantly improve one's mood and even result in feelings of elation when taken regularly. The ideal way to consume yerba mate is by making it into a tea, with water being heated to a boiling temperature and steeping the herb. Even for those who are recovering from borderline personality disorder can benefit from the consumption of yerba mate, as many attribute it to being an excellent natural pick-me-upper.

Kava Kava

Recognized as one of the best natural anti-anxiety herbs, kava kava is also used to treat fatigue and insomnia. The effects of kava kava are felt instantly, leaving you feeling calm and mellow. However, the consumption of kava kava should be restricted to less than 3 months as taking it too often may damage the liver. In order to avoid these side effects, kava kava may be taken for a short period when one begins treatment for borderline personality disorder. Kava kava should not be taken together with prescription drugs, although it may be used as a temporary alternative to antidepressants and benzodiazepines in the treatment of anxiety.

Valerian

Valerian has long been recognized for its ability to treat depression, anxiety, and insomnia. Those suffering from borderline personality disorder can benefit from its ability to calm the urge for self-harm. It acts as a sedative to the body's nerve centers, providing relief for pain and tension. Consuming valerian also results in more peaceful sleep because it calms the nervous system.

Valerian should not be taken in conjunction with sleep medication because it will further enhance its effects. The most effective way to enjoy the benefits of valerian is to take it in low doses, with intervals of two or three weeks. Valerian should be taken in small amounts mixed with other tea blends. Taking it in higher amounts may result in hallucinations as reported by some populations.

St. John's Wort

St. John's Wort is a plan that grows in the United States although its medicinal benefits have been known for centuries. Today it is widely recognized for its ability to help people stabilize moods. It is one of the most famous natural remedies used to supplement treatment in people with borderline personality disorder. It is also taken as alternative treatment for depression. Studies show that the effects of St. John's Wort are similar to the effects of antidepressants.

Chamomile

Chamomile is usually taken in the form of a tea to help people sleep better. Chamomile tea is recommended for those who have borderline personality disorder because it can help stabilize moods and help people calm down especially when they are feeling anxious and frustrated. Chamomile is milder than other kinds of herbs and may be best for those who are undergoing initial treatment although if you don't feel the effects right away you may need a stronger herb.

Chapter 16: Recovery

It is important for people who are diagnosed with borderline personality disorder to keep in mind that therapy is a process. Patience, hard work, and commitment are all necessary in order for therapy to work. Each time you are faced with a new skill, it is important that you approach this with an open mind. You may find that you'll be able to learn a new skill which will serve you the most good along the way especially when dealing with triggers and emotional responses.

During therapy, it is also normal for people with BPD to fall and sometimes get off track. As long as you get back on the path and stay on course despite the challenges you encounter along the way. If you find yourself feeling lost or lacking motivation, the best thing that you can do is talk to your therapist right away.

It is also important to change the way you view yourself, especially during treatment and recovery. Be kind, compassionate, and forgiving to yourself most of all. Accept the situation for all it's worth and take it as a learning curve. Remember that the skills you can learn from therapy will also serve a purpose later in life. You are not the one to blame for the problems you encounter but improving the situation lies in your own hands.

Part of the recovery process is transitioning back to your normal life once you have completed treatment. Your treatment center should be able to provide you with a helpful exit strategy to help you transition back into your home with as little problems as possible.

The world may seem different once you're in the recovery phase, as compared to how it seemed when you first started. However, keep in mind that this change in perception is positive. As you ease your way back into the world, group therapy may continue to be helpful because it helps you discover that you are not alone in your struggles. During recovery you are also encouraged to seek out support from social circles that are outside the treatment facility, such as reconnecting with old friends or forming new friendships out of healthy activities. Recovery will be made much smoother with the support of friends who share the same passions and interests as you do.

If you want to get back to work after recovery, your treatment center may be able to provide vocational support. Be open if you aren't sure where to start as they have the expertise to identify your strengths and build a career based on it. Ask for help from the treatment center, or from close friends and family on how to write a resume and cover letter that you can send out to job applications. The job search may bring about anxiety but you can overcome it by participating in individual and group therapy sessions. Similarly, if you want to go back to school you may also discuss this option with your treatment center.

Staying active will bring about tremendous benefits whether or not you have BPD. It is especially beneficial during the recovery stage as it helps maintain a healthy relationship with your body. Get involved in yoga, running, sports, and other forms of physical activity that you enjoy. It will not only keep you fit but also give you a sense of accomplishment and control over your body and mind. Physical activity is also an excellent outlet in case you encounter stressful situations.

Chapter 17: Emotional Triggers

People with borderline personality disorder have emotional triggers which are defined as situations that intensify symptoms. These triggers differ from one person to another although some triggers are common in most people who have BPD.

Triggers are classified into two categories: external and internal. External emotional triggers are those that happen outside of oneself while internal triggers are thoughts and feelings. Each time a person with borderline personality disorder experiences a trigger, a symptom of BPD will immediately intensify.

Common BPD emotional triggers include perceived or real abandonment, any kind of rejection, losing a job, anything that reminds them of a past traumatic experience, or ending a relationship. However, out of all of these, the most common trigger for those with BPD is perceived abandonment as well as rejection. Even in situations that seem mundane such as someone not responding to a call or text message can provoke a sense of abandonment and rejection for someone who is suffering from borderline personality disorder. It should be remembered that emotional triggers are individual experiences but for people whose loved ones have BPD, understanding these triggers is crucial in helping to minimize symptoms.

Relationship triggers are also common in borderlines. Events in their personal relationships that leave them feeling rejected, abandoned, or even mildly criticized can result in self-harm, impulsive behavior, and suicide.

Cognitive triggers such as thoughts that seem to come out of nowhere are also considered triggers for people with borderline personality disorder. Those who have suffered from childhood trauma or abuse are more prone to this type of emotional trigger. Simply remembering a past event can invoke extreme emotions. In fact the memory does not even have to be one that is negative for it to be an emotional trigger; a person with BPD may be reminded of times in the past which leads them to think that their present life is not as good anymore.

How To Manage Emotional Triggers

People with BPD oftentimes face difficulties in identifying the triggers that worsen their symptoms. While some people feel that these triggers come out of nowhere, the fact is that there are situations, places, or events that trigger their symptoms.

Here is a simple exercise that can help you manage emotional triggers:

1. Find a quiet place and sit down with a paper and pen, or write it on a computer if this makes you feel more comfortable. Take note that this exercise may cause you to feel some stress as it will encourage you to think about situations that may have provoked the symptoms of BPD. If this is the case, plan an activity afterwards that will soothe or relax you.

2. Create 3 columns and label them as: trigger, emotion, and response.

3. Try to remember the last incident that caused you to experience negative emotions such as feelings of anger, sadness, loneliness, emptiness, or shame. In the trigger column, list down events that happened right before you felt the negative emotions. Take into consideration that the trigger could be anything internal or external. It could be something that happened in your external environment such as having a small argument with a close friend. The trigger could also be something that happened mentally such as thinking of a positive or negative memory.

4. Under the "emotion" column, indicate exactly which emotional reaction the trigger provoked. You don't have to limit it to just one emotion, as it could be several, such as feeling anger and shame at the same time.

5. Next, indicate the response you had towards the emotion under the "response" column. For

example, if you felt anger as an emotion you may have resorted to an act of self-harm. Alternatively if you felt anger but was able to manage your response because of what you learned in therapy, record that as well.

6. Try to identify up to 3 experiences that occurred within the last two months which caused you to feel extreme emotions. Next, repeat steps 3 – 5 for these experiences.

7. Once you are done with the exercise, look at the column that is labeled "triggers". You may notice that there is a consistent pattern of events or experiences that cause your emotional triggers to begin.

8. Continue referring to this exercise in the future and writing down the responses you have to triggers you experience in the future.

9. As you continue to work with your list, you may be able to identify other events that tend to trigger you. Once you have more information about emotional triggers, you will be more skilled at coping with future episodes.

Dealing with Stress

Borderline Personality Disorder is also characterized by the inability to deal with stress effectively. It is one of the most notorious triggers but with the proper approach you can overcome stress.

Although stress is a common trigger in people with BPD, most individuals can be stressed out with the fact that they do not know when their symptoms will manifest themselves. To better understand stress as a trigger, you may want to consider having a diary or journal where you can take note of when you begin to feel episodes and identify the event that caused it.

Staying healthy is also necessary in overcoming stress as a trigger. You will be less prone to episodes and triggers if you are getting enough sleep, eating properly, and taking vitamins. Stress also has negative effects on the physical body which you can combat. When a person is experiencing stress, this releases cortisol in the brain, a compound that reduces the ability of the immune system to ward of illness. This means that stress makes you physically more prone to a host of other illnesses and can make you sick.

When you have a better understanding of exactly what causes your stress, you can take the extra step to simply avoid it. Many people tend to miss the obvious fact that you can indeed avoid stressful situations. For example if being around too many people stresses you out, spend more time in quiet locations or do your Christmas shopping early in the year.

How To Cope With Triggers

Although people with borderline personality disorder are prone to developing emotional triggers, also known as BPD episodes, these are manageable with the strategies listed below:

1. Once you have identified what events, situations, or experiences cause your triggers, the easiest way to cope with them is by avoiding them whenever possible. Although it is a given that some triggers will be easier to avoid than others, taking action to avoid other triggers can significantly reduce the incidences of emotional episodes. You should be responsible for identifying which triggers you can avoid. If you avoid every single thing, including people, this can lead to living a very limited life.

2. Gradually approaching your triggers as a way of facing your fears is a method that also works for other people with borderline personality disorder. Just because certain events trigger emotional responses in you doesn't mean that their effect will always be the same. For some people, facing their fears regularly helps them overcome it completely. If you would like to try this approach, try it with a small trigger first and work your way to the bigger ones.

3. Understanding which triggers tend to send you over the edge will help you come up with a plan to manage them more effectively. Each time one of your top triggers comes along, approach it with the coping skill that you wrote about in the

list described above. If you need to, go over the whole list until you have managed to get over the triggers completely.

4. People with borderline personality disorder tend to resort to dangerous activities when experiencing a BPD episode including violence, unsafe sex, and suicide. If you are prone to these types of impulses when you are going through an episode, you may want to talk to a therapist. While it is entirely possible to control these reactions, seeking professional help in the meantime can guide you through it in the safest way possible. Most importantly, you should remember that there is always someone willing to help you and that you are encouraged to ask for help when you need it.

Chapter 18: Employment And Coping With Love Ones

Many people who have personality disorders can still function properly to earn a living if they are receiving treatment. However, work can seem overwhelming and difficult if you are already struggling with a mental health illness. In extreme cases, borderline personality disorder may make it challenging to have a career and fight the illness simultaneously. If you are going through the struggle of employment, remember that treatment is crucial to having a successful career despite being diagnosed with BPD. Health should always come first especially if you want to be cured of a mental or personality disorder. Oftentimes, those suffering from BPD tend to forget that they are worthy of the best care possible, just like every other human being.

People with borderline personality disorder feel joy from helping other people, are also best suited for jobs that allow them to do this. This is because in reality, people with BPD can still be loving, caring individuals that are functioning members of society. Only when the illness is left untreated does it prevent people from being successful in both work and personal lives. Treatment must always be the first priority for every person who has borderline personality disorder.

If you want to take better care of yourself in the context of a job, remember the following:

1. Start a healthy routine that allows you to have time away to take care of your mind and body.

2. If you feel that you need a mental health day, speak up to your employer. Chances are they will be understanding of the situation especially if you have been upfront about your condition early on. It is understood that you cannot be a productive worker if you feel too stressed, anxious, or distracted.

3. Make sure that you participate in group therapy as part of your routine. No matter how hectic your work schedule is, it is crucial to always make time for treatment.

Coping with loved ones with BPD

At home

Here are some things for you to think about when approaching experiences with your loved one at home:

- Be as predictable and consistent as possible: If you tell your loved one that you will do something, it is important that you keep your word. Otherwise, you may find yourself as the recipient of a painful outburst of accusations, this may be difficult to handle but it is important to remember that those with BPD need a sense of stability and consistency in their lives. In the event that you aren't able to keep your word and you are lashed out upon, do not succumb to the outrage but instead apologize and start again.

- Encourage your loved one to be more responsible: Even if they are undergoing treatment, they may still end up participating in actions that will not benefit them. Whether it's in the form of racking up a dangerously high credit card bill or bumping a car, encourage responsibility and accountability by not bailing them out. Allow them to understand the repercussions of their actions without the use of painful words. It may help to have them use a credit card with a smaller limit rather than giving them complete liberty to use one with a high limit. Remember that if you keep rescuing them from their mistakes they won't have any motivation to change for the better.

- Give them honest feedback in all situations that they encounter: If your loved one thinks that they were treated unfairly, don't reinforce these negative thoughts unless you completely believe it to be true. Oftentimes, individuals with borderline personality disorder have no idea how their actions are affecting others. For example, if they end up getting fired because of their actions, empathize with them on the situation but don't agree with negative thoughts they may say, such as placing the blame on their coworkers. Instead, approach it with an empathic attitude and offer help on finding a solution.

- Avoid escalating arguments: Because people with borderline personality disorder are more sensitive, they may misinterpret what you say. You may say something with good intentions as a form of constructive criticism to which your loved one will respond to with harmful words. Instead of allowing such situations to grow into a full-blown argument, it is necessary for you to always keep your cool despite feeling frustrated and defeated.

Getting the whole family involved in the treatment of your relative with BPD can provide great benefits for everyone. It is common for family members to feel confused about understanding the disorder as a whole, as well as its symptoms and implications. Family members may also be easily overwhelmed by having to deal with the behavior of a relative who is borderline. Family therapy is effective in helping the entire unit understand BPD better, and learn practical methods in coping.

The symptoms of BPD can have negative effects on the family dynamic. Even worse, an already dysfunctional family may increase the severity of BPD symptoms in a person. These are crucial factors to remember if you have a family member suffering from the disorder. Family therapy is highly recommended for its benefits in identifying any cycles within the unit that may exacerbate symptoms of BPD in a person, thereby reducing the damage done to the patient as well as his family.

When family therapy is successful, BPD symptoms will be easily managed and the whole family can enjoy normal functioning. The end goal of family therapy is to encourage trust and support for the loved one with BPD, increasing their chances of recovery.

For You To Remember

Living with a person who has borderline personality disorder can be a daunting, exhausting job. Their mood swings, intense emotions, and need for reassurance can make your own life chaotic but it doesn't have to be.

- Just like with any other illness, learning as much as you can about borderline personality disorder will keep you informed on how you can continue caring for your loved one in the best way possible. Knowledge about BPD will be your most powerful weapon in dealing with the illness.

- Take care of yourself by spending some time each day doing something that makes you feel good. It is important for you to pay extra attention to yourself since living with someone who has BPD can feel like a full-time job. It would also be helpful if you had a therapist or a trusted circle of friends whom you can share the experiences with. While you are providing a form of moral support you shouldn't forget about being supported as well. Your local community may also be able to provide you with a support network of other people who are living with borderlines. Having a positive outlet will ensure that you continue providing the care that your loved one needs to get better.

- Be patient and persistent especially in the beginning when your loved one may resist the idea of getting treated. Provide them with the reassurance they need that you will be there for them and continue to support them until they are better. When they have appointments, it is also best to accompany them as a form of moral support.

Empathy For Borderlines

Practicing empathy towards loved ones with borderline personality disorder will provide them with tremendous moral support. It is often confused with sympathy, but empathy focuses on feeling what the other person is going through. An empathic attitude will make a person understand that they are not alone in their predicament. It will let them know that they are cared for, supported, and loved. In any relationship, empathy is an extremely important aspect but for those whose loved ones have BPD it is even more necessary.

However, practicing empathy can be difficult because as family and friends, you may find it hard to empathize with someone who is hurting other people and themselves due to the choices they are making. Their perspective of life is completely different from yours, and you may not be able to see any logic in their actions. While being empathic doesn't mean that you have to agree with all their choices, it requires listening to them, spending time with them, and making an effort to understand their point of view. It is a grand way of showing respect to a loved one with borderline personality disorder.

Here are some ways you can practice empathy to support a loved one with BPD:

1. Listen to them and be 100% focused on the moment. When talking, don't hold your phone, shut off the television, and listen as attentively as you can. Try to determine how the other person is feeling by observing their body language, and the change in their tone of voice. If you aren't sure what they mean, asking them to expound further will show that you are really paying attention to what they are saying.

2. Choose your words before responding in the conversation. Try to absorb the gravity and meaning behind what has just been said before providing a response. Information comes to people quickly nowadays, and most people don't think about what they say. For the person with BPD, words can be a trigger as they are more sensitive. It is necessary for their loved ones to think about the effect of their words once spoken.

3. Acknowledge that you are listening and validate it by saying words like "I understand". This may be complemented by nodding or by a gentle touch. This kind of behavior while communicating can help reduce feelings of vulnerability in the speaker.

4. Show your support by letting your loved one with BPD know that you are there for them. Express that you are there for them and willing to help. You can take it one level higher by offering to work on it as a partnership and telling them that you'd like to work through it with them together.

5. Respect the person by expressing that you understand it can be difficult to discuss what they are going through. Recognize their efforts by telling them you think they are doing a good job at coping with it. Additionally, tell them that they are an important person with goals to accomplish and that being diagnosed with borderline personality disorder does not define who they are or limit the opportunities available to them.

6. Be aware of your body language when talking to a loved one with BPD. Show respect by maintaining eye contact as they voice out their concerns, feelings, and fears. Keep them engaged through body language. Nodding as they speak shows that you are absorbing what they say and understanding what they mean.

Reacting To People With Borderline Personality Disorder

If a close friend or loved one has BPD, you may find yourself as the recipient to outburst and extreme emotions. This may cause you to feel hurt or be angry at the person, but giving in to these emotions may damage your relationship.

Drama is a predominant theme in relationships with individuals who have BPD, whether they are a friend, coworker, spouse, child, or relative. When dealing with them it is important that you are able to manage your own emotions so as not to add fuel to the fire.

It is also crucial that you realize people with BPD oftentimes cannot help their emotions if they are not receiving treatment. People who have close relationships with those who have BPD usually take responsibility for solving their problems. However, this kind of codependent relationship will not benefit either of you and most especially will not help them improve their symptoms. A codependence will prevent the establishment of healthy boundaries and will also prevent both of you from maximizing your potential as individuals. You may want to take a step back to examine how your own emotions and reactions could be complicating the relationship.

While harmony may not be permanent in your relationship with someone who has BPD, you can do your part to reduce conflict and drama. The primary way of going about this is by improving your communication skills in every encounter with them.

If your goal is to address negative actions or behavior in someone who has borderline personality disorder, avoid using "you" and instead focus on "I" statements. When you avoid "you" statements, you are preventing someone with BPD from reacting with defensiveness. By communicating this way, you show that you are taking ownership of the problem rather than simply blaming them for it. However, remember that even when positively using "I" statements, your loved one could still hear "you" statements. Be patient and give them time to adjust to your communication skills. Continue being consistent in the way you approach and talk to them, and you will see improvements in no time.

People with borderline personality disorder are paranoid and often feel like they are being attacked even when they are not. Because of their sensitivity, they may resort to rage when they think that others are not listening to them. Keep in mind that the concerns or complaints of someone with borderline personality disorder may seem petty, but it is up to you to turn the conversation from a lose-lose situation to a win-win one by reacting the right way.

If you think that you are not contributing in improving the situation, you may want to consider therapy or participating in support groups.

Chapter 19: Famous People with BPD

Although borderline personality disorder is a mental health illness that causes emotional instability and other behavioral issues, it should not prevent one from contributing as a functional member of society. In fact, many famous people have also been diagnosed with BPD but have been able to make significant contributions to the entertainment industry.

1. Angelina Jolie is a world-famous American actress, author, and film director. She is one of the highest paid actresses in Hollywood, according to Forbes magazine. During the late 1990's, she suffered from suicidal and homicidal tendencies which prompted her to admit herself into a psychiatric institution. Despite these tendencies she had no plan of actually carrying out her plans. Angelia Jolie was diagnosed with presumptive borderline personality disorder but has been able to effectively overcome it today.

2. The late Amy Winehouse was a famous English singer and songwriter. Her battle with substance abuse was known around the world, and received a lot of media attention. In 2005, Amy Winehouse was on the news for her severe mood swings, sudden weight loss, alcoholism and drug abuse. She also admitted battling depression, resorting to self-harm and eating

disorders. In 2008 she was able to get rid of her drug habit, which was unfortunately replaced by extreme alcoholism. She died one morning in July 2011 from a relapse and alcohol poisoning.

3. Lindsay Lohan is an American artist, actress, and model. She had her career path paved out for her when she was just three years old when she was child model. But during her adult years she received media attention for cocaine abuse and constantly getting into car accidents and was also sent to a drug rehabilitation center for driving under the influence. Lindsay Lohan also spent some time in jail, all of which are characteristics of extreme borderline personality disorder.

4. Britney Spears is a famous American singer, entertainer, and actress. She is notorious for her many impulsive acts that landed her on television and magazines around the world. These included shaving her head bald, and marrying her childhood friend Jason Alexander and filing for annulment after just 55 hours. She was admitted to drug rehabilitation centers many times over.

5. The late Courtney Love is an American singer, actress, and author. For most of her life she battled substance abuse particularly cocaine and opiates. In 2003, Courtney Love was arrested for smashing the windows of her boyfriend's apartment while under the influence of drugs.

She was also admitted into treatment facilities numerous times for abuse of alcohol and drugs.

Conclusion

Mental illnesses such as borderline personality disorder unfortunately carry a lot of stigma with it. Those who suffer from psychiatric illnesses are referred to as crazy or incapable of living normal lives. These terms are merely misconceptions and should never be used to describe a loved one with BPD because it can affect their lives.

The leading cause of death from psychiatric illnesses is a lack of education and awareness, negative reactions from their loved ones, and the inability to get treatment. In this book we hope that you have understood the impact of all these aspects in the life of someone who has BPD, especially the importance for them to receive the proper treatment. Just like any other person who has an illness, a person with borderline personality disorder has all the right in the world to obtain quality treatment and therapy to recover from BPD.

The best way for loved ones to cope is to keep themselves informed about borderline personality disorder, such as the information we have provided in this book. You may encounter them at home, in your personal relationships, and in the work place. Regardless of where they are in your life, there is a proper way of addressing them that will encourage positive change.

Lightning Source UK Ltd.
Milton Keynes UK
UKHW01f1753150618
324323UK00001B/12/P

9 781508 865476